A Handbook for Lunchtime Supervisors

and their Managers

David Fulton Publishers

David Fulton Publishers Ltd
The Chiswick Centre, 414 Chiswick High Road, London W4 5TF

www.fultonpublishers.co.uk
www.onestopeducation.co.uk

First published in Great Britain in 2006 by David Fulton Publishers

10 9 8 7 6 5 4 3 2 1

David Fulton Publishers is a division of Granada Learning Limited.

British Library Cataloguing in Publication Data
A catalogue record for this book is available from the British Library.

ISBN: 1 84312 068 2

Typeset by FiSH Books, Enfield, Middx.
Printed and bound in Great Britain

Contents

For my parents for teaching me so much

About the author

For the last ten years I have been training school staff, mainly lunchtime supervisors and teaching assistants. I became interested in the work of LTSs some years ago when my son's excellent childminder told me about her 'other job' as a senior lunchtime supervisor at a local primary school in which, at that time, she had received no training. As a qualified social worker and ChildLine counsellor with many years' experience, I have an evangelical commitment to the importance of valuing and communicating with children. I am also convinced that everyone working with children needs training and support. With the help of a local head teacher I piloted a training package for primary school LTSs which I have since refined and delivered to many schools.

When I originally started this work, support staff were rarely given a voice or offered training. Thankfully this is changing. The hundreds of lunchtime supervisors I have worked with (in and outside the playground) have taught me how challenging, stressful and exciting their role can be.

Shirley Rose
London
January 2006

Acknowledgements

Many professional colleagues, friends and family members have helped in the writing of this book. Without their support and feedback, I doubt it would have been possible. I would especially like to acknowledge the help over the years provided by Peter Gordon and for his brilliant insight from the manager's viewpoint; the good natured and efficient assistance and feedback from Yvonne Rose (not to mention her impressive knowledge of punctuation); the unstinting support, input and encouragement of John Crowther. I thank Louis Crowther for occasionally getting off my computer and Simon Crowther for getting on it and becoming my IT expert.

I would also like to thank Jenny Bloom for her early years' advice, and Tracey Ridley for her health and safety input. I am grateful to Helen Ford and Viv Levy for listening to my moans, and to the Friday morning coffee group for encouragement and caffeine.

I am particularly indebted to the hundreds of lunchtime supervisors who have moved, enthralled and inspired me with their experiences, and to the many head teachers and school managers with whom I have worked over the years.

Introduction

A brief history of the lunchtime supervisor

In 1906 Parliament was successfully persuaded that hungry children had trouble learning, and the Provision of School Meals Act came into force, permitting local authorities to provide school meals. By 1939, less than 50 per cent of local authorities were providing this service for which families paid 2d (1p) for a meal unless entitled to free lunches. For many years teachers were required as part of their duties to supervise children at lunchtime. In 1968, following a long struggle, teachers won the right to have their own lunchtime break, although many continued to supervise lunchtime on a voluntary basis in return for a free school meal. Lunchtime supervisors were employed by schools prior to 1968, although their numbers and importance increased dramatically over the next few decades.

The role of the lunchtime supervisor

Schools organise the supervision of lunchtime in a variety of ways. The majority employ supervisors specifically to work for a short period in the middle of each day. Some schools require their teaching assistants to cover lunchtime duties, whilst others use a mixture of teaching assistants and lunchtime supervisors. Many of the issues outlined in this book are also relevant for teaching assistants undertaking lunchtime duties.

As LTSs (as I will refer to you from now on), you have an important part to play in the success of the school day. Anyone who works in school will know that if the lunchtime goes well, teaching staff and children benefit and the afternoon is likely to run smoothly. When the lunchtime break goes wrong, picking up the pieces can be time consuming, disruptive and stressful.

LTSs are usually required to supervise children for approximately an hour and a quarter per day, to ensure that they have lunch, and the opportunity to play and let off steam. You are also involved in many important aspects of children's school experience including their eating, playing, friendship groups, behaviour and safety.

Staff who feel valued at work are more likely to develop higher self-esteem and motivation. This has not always been the case for LTSs and throughout this book ways to include and support you will be explored.

From a management point of view

Managers will be aware that the lunchtime break is now being given greater importance. Ofsted inspections include an assessment of the behaviour of the pupils during lunchtime, and many schools accept they must put in the resources to ensure this part of the day is successful.

Until recently, relatively little has been written by the government about the role of the LTS. In September 2005, as part of the behaviour and attendance pilot, a primary national strategy professional development pack was produced entitled *Playtimes and Lunchtimes* (DfES 2005a). This examines the contribution that well-managed playtimes and lunchtimes can make to children's social, emotional and behavioural development. It also puts playtimes and lunchtimes into the context of a whole school behaviour policy, promotes practical strategies, and considers the needs of staff who supervise this part of the school day.

Very often head teachers express genuine concern about the difficulties LTSs face. They voice the desire to have an empowered and skilled team of staff who use their initiative to constructively manage behaviour so that problems do not escalate or spill into the classroom. To achieve this, many head teachers now recognise that LTSs need to be provided with training and support.

What is in this book?

This book is for primary school lunchtime supervisors and their managers. It explores the necessary support, training and skills that LTSs require to do their job well, and looks at whole school practices that can contribute to happy lunchtimes and lunchtime staff. It includes examples of excellent practice developed in a range of primary schools, and provides case studies and exercises to highlight how difficulties and pitfalls can be overcome.

The book is divided into two parts. The first part is for LTSs, although it is relevant for managers too. It comprises ten chapters described below, plus one shorter appendix focusing on LTSs' future learning and career development. The second part of the book is particularly relevant for those who line manage LTSs and for senior managers responsible for the lunchtime break. It provides notes and good practice guidelines on each of the chapters (notes on Chapters 4 and 5 have been amalgamated due to the overlap in subject matter).

Also included in each chapter are activities which LTSs can do alone or with other members of the staff team. Managers may wish to use these activities in training sessions or meetings to develop their team's knowledge and skills. LTSs will need to feel comfortable enough to explore issues honestly and openly.

The chapters in the book are set out as follows:

Part 1 is for lunchtime supervisors to read:

- Chapter 1 explores the LTS's role and responsibilities within primary schools.
- Chapter 2 discusses the development of communication systems within the school to ensure relevant information is appropriately shared between LTSs and relevant others.
- Chapter 3 focuses on how LTSs can build positive relationships with children.
- Chapter 4 tackles ways LTSs can promote positive behaviour in the playground and in the dining room.
- Chapter 5 looks at managing challenging behaviour at lunchtime, and how this can be part of the whole school behaviour plan.
- Chapter 6 explores the problem of bullying at lunchtime.
- Chapter 7 is about the importance of play, and how to organise and initiate playground activities.
- Chapter 8 focuses on how to manage wet play.
- Chapter 9 looks at keeping children safe at lunchtime.
- Chapter 10 discusses the role of the LTS in relation to child protection.
- The appendix outlines further learning and career development for LTSs.

Part 2 provides managers' notes, divided by chapters. These are provided to help managers to fulfil their responsibilities, to support LTSs effectively, and help them prepare training sessions.

Part 1 – Information for lunchtime supervisors

CHAPTER 1

The role and responsibilities of the lunchtime supervisor

Introduction

The lunchtime supervisor's work may be challenging and rewarding, but rarely boring. As well as ensuring that children have lunch, and the opportunity to play, skilled LTSs are helping, and often teaching, children to eat, to play, to socialise, to co-exist and to deal with conflict and friendships. In other words, you are encouraging children to become rounded and civilised human beings. LTSs are required to keep large numbers of children safe, to manage their behaviour, to listen and respond to their problems (which may at times be serious). You are required to initiate and sustain play, to tolerate severe weather conditions, to prevent and respond to accidents, to be aware of bullying, and to be sensitive to cultural and social issues.

What are your main responsibilities?

ACTIVITY 1

Your role

List the main tasks you are required to do:

1   To keep children safe in the playground

2

3

4

5

6

7

8

Get together with other team members and compile a team list.

Your tasks are likely to include:

- Supervising the children in the playground and dining room
- Managing children's behaviour
- Keeping children safe
- Setting up the lunch area, and clearing the dining room at the end of lunchtime
- Supervising children whilst they are queuing and eating
- Listening to children
- Recognising and responding to bullying and child abuse
- Responding to disputes and fights between children
- Assisting isolated or distressed pupils
- Responding to illness, accidents and emergencies
- Administering basic first aid
- Encouraging children to play constructively by initiating, sustaining and at times joining in with games
- Being responsible for playground equipment
- Supervising wet play
- Liaising with teachers and informing them about good and bad behaviour

Clarifying your responsibilities

To be effective at work, you will need to be clear about your role and responsibilities. New LTSs often describe 'being thrown in at the deep end' and 'learning on the job'. To clarify your position, it may help to:

*   *Obtain a job description outlining your duties and responsibilities. If you do not have one, ask your line manager for assistance.*
*   *Find out what other relevant guidelines are available. Schools may have prepared an induction pack for LTSs or a written outline of your duties.*
*   *Ask about what is expected of you. The senior LTS or experienced colleagues can instruct you and answer your questions. If you are unclear, do not be afraid to ask.*

ACTIVITY 2

Try to obtain a relevant job description if you have not already been given one.

Job descriptions can be updated so talk to your line manager if you think changes need to be made.

The main responsibilities of the LTS

Keeping children safe

One of your most important duties is to keep children safe at lunchtime by maintaining order in the dining room and playground. You are also required to keep children safe from abuse and bullying. All schools will have a range of relevant policies outlining your responsibilities in relation to health and safety, child protection and anti-bullying which will be discussed in greater detail in Chapters 6, 7 and 10.

Caring for children

Many LTSs describe how they care for the children in the way they would like their own children to be cared for. It is not unusual for younger children to call you 'mum' in error, and in one school the LTSs were nicknamed 'the dinner mummies'. Although you are not solely in a parental role, nurturing and supporting children are important parts of your job. You are also likely to be the person who deals with children's injuries and accidents, as well as distress or ill health. It is not surprising that, if you listen well and develop positive relationships with pupils, you are likely to be told their problems and secrets. This will be explored further in future chapters.

Instructing children

As an LTS you have the potential to be an excellent instructor or educator. For example, for a range of social or cultural reasons, when children start school they may never have learnt to use a knife or fork or to eat at a table. You can sensitively teach a child to 'do things differently'. You can also teach children to share, to take turns, to negotiate and to express their emotions appropriately. How often do you find yourself reminding children to deal with conflict without resorting to violence? You can't wave a magic wand and *make* children get on, but you can teach them how to talk about their differences, to explore options, and to agree on a solution. LTSs regularly teach children how to play safely, to respect each other's cultures and customs, to empathise and to generally get along together.

Accountability

To whom are you accountable?

Every member of staff in a school is accountable to somebody else. To do the job well it will help to know who decides on your role and responsibilities. This is usually the head teacher or a senior manager, although the school governors will also have some say. This person will be referred to as your *line manager* from now on.

The role of the senior lunchtime supervisor

There may be a senior LTS who acts as an intermediary between the line manager and the team. The senior LTS may also have management responsibility including the preparation and implementation of rotas, dealing with the most challenging behaviour, induction of new staff, and staff development.

ACTIVITY 3

Accountability

In pairs or in larger groups answer the following questions:

1　In what sort of situations do you feel the need to consult with a more senior colleague?

2　Who is your line manager?

3　Who determines your duties and work patterns?

4　Who do you go to when you have a personal problem which affects work?

5　Who do you ask when you are unsure of something?

6　Who do you go to when you are worried about a child who appears to be distressed?

7　To whom do you report a child's unacceptable behaviour?

8　If a child is not eating on a regular basis, who would you tell?

9　With whom do you share ideas for changing or improving work practice?

Each school will organise things differently. It may be that you are expected to talk to the senior LTS, or you may be required to go straight to the class teacher or the head teacher. What matters is that you are clear and happy about the school's expectations.

ACTIVITY 4

Dilemmas:

When working with teachers and other members of the school staff there are likely to be areas where responsibility is unclear. Lack of clarity can result in frustration and bad feelings.

Discuss these real life dilemmas in your team and decide who is responsible in each of the following situations.

- Children had been told to remain in the dining room at lunchtime 'on detention' for bad behaviour that occurred in a morning lesson. Who is responsible for supervising the children?
- It is a cold winter day and some children come into the playground without their coats. Who is responsible for ensuring that they wear their coats?
- Your own son had started as a pupil in reception. Should he be with you throughout the lunchtime, as he wants?
- Who decides about the use of playground equipment, and whether children can use the grassy area of the playground?
- A child is sick in the toilet. Who is responsible for clearing it up?
- A teacher fails to collect her class from the playground at the end of lunchtime. It is time for you to go home. Who should supervise the children?
- A 'difficult' parent insists on waiting outside the playground at lunchtime and passes sweets to her children through the fence. Who is responsible for challenging her?

There may be other dilemmas that your team are struggling with. If so what are they? Discuss your concerns with your line manager.

Discussion points from the above activity

Dilemma 1

If you are supervising the dining room then you are responsible for all children's well-being. LTSs and teaching staff should discuss the practicalities of supervising children who have been placed in detention.

Dilemma 2

It is your responsibility to ensure children are wearing their coats. The class teacher may also share this with you.

Dilemma 3

LTSs whose own children attend the same school often agree that team colleagues will deal with the child/children whenever possible. This avoids accusations of favouritism, or concerns that the LTS is too busy caring for their own child to do their job properly. It is also better for the child.

Dilemma 4

A decision about the use of equipment and the use of the grassy area in the playground is ultimately a senior management decision. Ideally you will be able to have your say.

Dilemma 5

Responsibility for cleaning up vomit or other accidents will vary between schools. Many LTSs have this as part of their duties, although some do not.

Dilemma 6

You are responsible for the children's safety until they are in the care of another responsible adult. You will have to stay with the children until another member of staff relieves you. The teacher's lateness will need to be tackled by a senior manager.

Dilemma 7

You may choose to politely challenge the parent. If you feel unsafe or concerned, you should request backup from a senior manager.

Do you feel valued?

In your role as an LTS, it is crucial that you are valued and respected by members of the school community, including the teaching staff and the children. Schools will vary in the treatment of support staff and the systems they may have to raise your status. You also have an important part to play in gaining the respect of others by being open and professional and by communicating your needs assertively. If you are unhappy with the way you are being treated, try to find a positive way to express your concerns, and say what you think could improve the situation. Good practice in this area will be described throughout this book.

If you would like to find out more about ways schools can raise your status see Notes for managers, page 100.

Confidentiality

Everybody who works in school needs to be aware of the importance of confidentiality. This means sharing certain information only with appropriate people. In schools, confidentiality can be complex. Every situation is different, and your action or inaction may have serious consequences. As part of a school staff team you are likely to be trusted with confidential information about the children you work with on a 'need to know' basis. This means that decisions are made, usually by a member of the senior management team, concerning who needs to know specific pieces of sensitive information about individual children and their families. All school employees have a professional responsibility to avoid sharing confidential information with anyone outside school unless they have been authorised to do so, and to avoid gossiping.

As LTSs you have the potential to form very close relationships with children, who may trust you with their personal problems. It is not unusual for young children to tell LTSs their concerns including embarrassingly intimate or worrying details about their family life. You may also notice changes in children's behaviour or marks on their bodies. If you have any concerns about a child's well-being, it is your responsibility to pass this information on to an appropriate person. This will be discussed in detail in Chapter 10.

LTSs often live near the school, and have strong community links. You may have worked at the school for many years, or be a parent of children at your workplace. This can have advantages and disadvantages. LTSs talk of the pleasure of being greeted in the street or supermarket by friendly children and parents. On other occasions they describe the pressures of being quizzed or angrily confronted by parents when they are off duty.

In such situations it is important to control your personal feelings and to respond calmly and professionally. Avoid entering into arguments with the parents as this usually makes matters worse. Explain firmly that you are not currently at work, and if they would like to discuss things further they should arrange to see the class teacher or head teacher.

ACTIVITY 5

Confidentiality questionnaire

Discuss these situations in groups or pairs and decide what you would say or do:

- You are at the local supermarket on Saturday and a parent from the school tells you she is worried that her daughter's class teacher is picking on her.
- A child tells you her dad is hitting her mum. The child asks you not to tell anyone else.
- You are in the playground after school collecting your own child when another mum asks you if her child is eating her dinner.
- You are in the playground after school when a dad asks you why his son is behaving like a sissy and playing girls' games at lunchtime.
- Another LTS who knows that you have access to children's records (from your work in the office) asks you if a particular child has a social worker.
- A parent verbally threatens you in the street and accuses you of hurting her child when you stopped a playground fight.

Giving information to parents

LTSs are frequently asked questions by parents about their children's behaviour or food intake. Some schools are happy for you to answer simple queries as long as the situation appears to be 'straightforward'. Others clearly expect you to direct the parent to the class teacher or head teacher. Talk to your line manager about your school's expectations in relation to Activity 5.

Conclusion

Your role is complex. Being clear about your school's expectations will help you to behave in a professional and confident manner. This in turn is likely to lead to greater job satisfaction, and more respect from others.

CHAPTER 2

Communication systems within the school

Introduction

In this chapter we will consider systems of communication within the school. There will be a number of practical activities to help you develop your thinking and skills. In the light of your short working hours, very specific tailor-made systems of communication need to be created to ensure you are well briefed, and that you pass on appropriately information to others.

Information about the school

How informed do you feel about what is happening at school, and how do you find out about rule changes or events? In the worst scenario, do you learn about these changes from the children? How often are you introduced to new members of office or teaching staff, or told when people are leaving? Many schools have developed excellent systems of communication to avoid such difficulties.

Below are examples highlighting when things have gone wrong.

CASE STUDY 1

A team of LTSs complained bitterly when they were not told about the staff Christmas lunch believing that, as they were not informed, they were not welcome. Their line manager was extremely apologetic and assured them this had been the result of stressed staff and inadequate communication systems, rather than deliberate exclusion.

CASE STUDY 2

A group of LTSs were exasperated when they were the only ones who came to school on an October Friday *not* wearing jeans. The whole school had decided to participate in a special fundraising 'Jeans for Genes day' without their knowledge.

ACTIVITY 1

Discuss within your team:

- How well are you informed about the day-to-day running of the school?
- What systems are in place to inform you about important events?

Information about children

To work effectively with children you will need to be provided with an appropriate level of information about their health, diet, family circumstances and special educational needs. As described in the previous chapter, this information may be confidential and so shared only on a 'need to know' basis.

ACTIVITY 2

Discuss the following case studies.

CASE STUDY 1

In a training session one LTS described how she couldn't understand why a year 3 girl kept ignoring her instructions, until she was informed by another child that the girl was deaf. What systems could be in place to ensure such information is shared appropriately?

CASE STUDY 2

A supervisor asked a seven-year-old boy why he looked sad. The boy's classmates informed her that his father had committed suicide some weeks earlier. How could this information have been shared more effectively?

Information to be shared about children may include:

- A list of children's special medical needs, displayed in a confidential place.
- An up-to-date list of children's special dietary requirements, placed in an appropriately accessible place.
- Sufficient details about children's special educational needs. This may be discussed in meetings or communicated in writing.
- Information about children who are bullying or are being bullied.
- Strategies for managing children with particularly challenging behaviour.
- Particular circumstances that may be affecting children including family problems (short term and long term).

ACTIVITY 3

Discuss the questions below:

- How well informed do you feel about the children you work with?
- What further information would help you to do your job better?
- What arrangements could be created to aid communication?

Communication systems

Effective communication systems include:

- Regular meetings with a range of relevant people
- Joint training and consultation for all staff
- Sufficient and relevant written communication
- Structured verbal communication
- Handover systems before and after lunchtime
- Feedback following 'serious incidents'

Meetings

Meetings can be time consuming and difficult to organise during your limited working hours. Your school may have opted for a system where the senior LTS and the head teacher or line manager meet on a regular basis to share information which is then passed on to you. Many LTS teams also meet with their line manager to share information, to review practice, to feed back on difficulties and successes, and to discuss training needs and school developments.

Many schools fix meetings on a regular termly or half-termly basis for approximately 30 minutes, usually immediately before or after lunchtime duties. LTSs are often, but not always, paid overtime to attend.

Prior to a meeting, you should be encouraged to contribute to the agenda and to raise issues of importance. Not everyone talks in meetings, and sometimes LTSs feel it is not their place to express an opinion. You are an important member of the school community who has a right to have your say. Once your team and your line manager have agreed to meet, it may help if you share the responsibility for making the meetings happen. To ensure that decisions made in meetings are acted upon, you should keep notes and refer to these at your next meeting.

If you are not having meetings, or you are not being paid to meet, raise this with your line manager. If decisions made at your meetings are not put into action, find an appropriate way to voice your concerns.

The role of the line manager as a 'go between'

As demonstrated by the case study below, following the meeting your line manager will be able to liaise between you and other staff groups to pass on concerns, feedback or requests.

> In a meeting with their line manager (the deputy head teacher), a group of LTSs expressed frustration that teachers were allowing children to come into the school building for lunchtime clubs without informing them. Also, LTSs were not being told which children required an early lunch. The line manager agreed to remind teachers to give LTSs the appropriate lists of names and reinforce the rules in relation to children coming into the school building at lunchtime (a card system). At future LTS meetings progress on these areas was monitored.

The meeting as a forum for building team relationships

You may be working in a team, often under pressure with little support or management. This can result in low morale and conflict between staff members. Anyone who has worked in 'unhappy teams' will know how unpleasant it can be. The case study below shows an example of a team who needed help to move on.

During a training session a senior LTS voiced her concerns about a breakdown in team relationships resulting from a bitter disagreement between two team members. This was clearly interfering with their effectiveness as a number of LTSs were refusing to talk to each other or even to sit around the same table. Following unsuccessful attempts to resolve their differences, the team agreed that they would seek help from their line manager. A meeting was called to air differences and to agree on acceptable behaviour whilst at work.

If you are struggling with similar issues, find a trusted person to assist you and your team. Although such discussions can be difficult, they can also be extremely productive.

Meetings without the line manager

You might meet on occasions as a team without your line manager to review your work and to support each other. This will need to be agreed by senior management subject to money being available to pay overtime.

Meetings with other staff members

In some schools, LTSs meet with the class teacher in the first few months of the school year for a short period to share relevant information about the children in the class.

If you have special responsibility for the nursery and reception pupils (foundation stage), the infant pupils (key stage 1) or the junior pupils (key stage 2), meetings may be specially arranged for these groups. You may also benefit from occasional meetings with the special educational needs coordinator (SENCO) to discuss how best to respond to children with special needs or behavioural problems.

The use of INSET to clarify rules, routines and policy

Many schools use INSET training days to offer staff the opportunity for joint training and consultation. Sessions may focus on school rules, routines and policies, and encourage staff groups to discuss their expectations to ensure consistent practice. Sometimes LTSs describe feeling unwelcome or intimidated by the idea of attending whole staff training. However, if the subject is relevant, you may be able to offer some valuable ideas.

A group of LTSs expressed their frustration at being required to sort out equipment cupboards on INSET days, whilst teaching staff discussed more important issues. The LTSs voiced their concerns and it was agreed that they would be invited to relevant sessions. The next INSET day focused on playground behaviour.

ACTIVITY 4

School meetings

Discuss the following questions briefly:

- How often do you meet with your line manager?
- If meetings are *not* happening, would you like this to change?
- Who decides on dates and times of meetings?
- Do meetings take place at the agreed date or time? If not, do the LTSs request them?
- Do you have an agenda and if so do you contribute to it?
- Do you meet *without* your line manager to review your work practices? If not, would this be helpful?
- Do you ever meet with other members of staff, for example the SENCO, to discuss children with special needs? If not, would this be helpful?
- Do you attend whole staff INSET training when relevant?

Written communication

Access to adequate written communication may include:

- The school newsletter for *all* LTSs – not just those of you who are also parents at the school
- Lists of dates of school terms, INSET days and other events
- Minutes from relevant meetings including those that you were unable to attend
- A message or briefing book where information is written by teaching staff about children's needs or difficulties
- Lists of children's allergies, medical and dietary needs
- Information/staff briefings written on a daily basis
- Lists of children attending lunchtime clubs, outings, etc.
- The detention book
- Forms, slips or books that enable information to be passed between LTSs and other staff
- Copies of guidelines outlining relevant policy and procedures

Communication systems require the cooperation of all staff members. Written information needs to be accessible, relevant, up to date and, when necessary, confidential.

Conclusion

Schools are extremely busy and complex places and special attention will need to be given to developing systems of communication. For the lunchtime to be a positive part of the day and for LTSs to feel included, a large amount of relevant information must be shared. In this chapter a range of systems and practices have been explored and examples of good practice have been highlighted.

Building positive relationships with children

Introduction

As a lunchtime supervisor you are often in an excellent position to build relationships with children. Unlike teaching staff, you have opportunities to play with and talk to children during the less structured parts of the day. If you succeed in developing positive relationships with the children, you are more likely to manage their behaviour constructively, and to become an important person in their school life.

In this chapter the necessary skills for building positive relationships will be explored, including ways to gain children's trust, how to listen, how to be child-centred, and how to help children cope with their emotions. It will also discuss how to find the correct balance between fun and firmness, how to become a positive role model, and the factors that interfere with building positive relationships with children.

How do you build positive relationships with children?

ACTIVITY 1

List a number of ways you already develop positive relationships with the children you work with.

1

2

3

4

5

6

These might include some of the following:

● Learning their names

● Being child-centred

● Offering praise and showing children that you have confidence in them

● Appearing and sounding positive

● Listening

● Responding sensitively to what you hear

● Being consistent, firm and fair

● Being a positive role model

These issues will be discussed below.

Learning names

Using a child's correct name is a way to reach out to them. Calling children 'sweetheart' or other such names is not quite so personal. Learning names takes time, depending on your memory and on the size of the school. In multicultural communities children might have less familiar names and remembering these with the correct pronunciation demonstrates your respect. LTSs often know the names of children who misbehave. There are a range of games that you can play with the children to help to learn their names. These include being tested by the child on a daily basis until you get their name correct or playing guessing games with the help of clues.

Being child-centred

When doing Activity 1, you may have included examples of being child-centred. This involves understanding what is happening from the child's point of view. It is not always easy to be child-centred, especially when child's behaviour makes you angry or frustrated.

ACTIVITY 2

Becoming child-centred

Think of a particular age group of children that you work with and try to answer the following questions below:

- Can you remember being this age?
- Have you had children or family members of your own, who have been this age?
- What do these children find interesting?
- What sort of ideas and communication can they understand?
- What do they find amusing?
- What worries them?
- What matters to them?
- How do these children get on with their classmates?
- How different are the boys and the girls?
- How do children of this age cope with children who are from other cultures?

If you wish to learn more about child development there are many books, articles and television programmes that your SENCO or other experts could recommend.

Examples of child-centred behaviour
- Talking to children about what interests them
- Sharing *appropriate* information about yourself
- Using humour carefully
- Playing and joining in with games
- Accepting children 'warts and all'
- Showing children that you can understand and help them to cope with their feelings
- Using the appropriate touch

Talking to children about what is of interest to them
When you get to know children you will learn about the games and music they enjoy, their favourite TV programmes, their friendship groups, family holidays and festivals, and probably many other personal details! As a child-centred LTS you will try to show interest in what matters to the children and encourage them to talk about

their world. You will speak in a way that children can understand, whilst being sensitive to their family circumstances and culture.

Sharing appropriate information about yourself

Many LTSs choose to share information about themselves and their family. This can be a helpful way to engage children's interest that helps you to become real to them. LTSs may choose to tell children about times in their own life when they experienced difficulties at school. This is usually intended to help children to feel that their worries are understood. However, care should be taken to avoid unnecessarily burdening or worrying children. It may be unhelpful, for instance, to talk about a painful illness or death in your family as the child is likely to sense your distress. Similarly, think carefully before talking about your own personal beliefs.

> Following the death of a child's grandparent, an LTS attempted to comfort her by saying 'Granny has gone to heaven'. She later realised that this had been inappropriate, as the child's family may not share a belief in heaven. In such situations, be guided by the child.

Using humour

When we use humour appropriately with children, we are saying 'I like you and I want to be playful'. It helps to lighten a situation, and laughter is well known for its psychological benefits. Obviously we need to be sensitive about the type of humour, and the words we use. Avoid sarcasm as it can be extremely confusing, and can also damage self-esteem. Children of various ages and experiences will react to humour very differently. A comment that a six-year-old might find funny, could be offensive or embarrassing to a ten-year-old. You will also need to know when to change tack, and when to respond firmly.

Playing and joining in with their games when you can

Many of the most enthusiastic LTSs describe the pleasure of joining in and having fun with children. This will be discussed in detail in Chapter 7.

Accepting children – warts and all

Children can be funny, spontaneous and loving. They can also be selfish, unkind, cheat and tell lies. This is normal behaviour, but can leave us feeling angry or appalled. The real task is to try to accept that children behave in negative ways, often for a range of reasons. Your role, therefore, is to help children to deal with their emotions more positively.

LTSs describe feeling furious when children lie. You may have witnessed a child's involvement in a playground incident, only to be told minutes later by the offender 'It wasn't me'. It may help if you can view this as an immature way of wriggling out of trouble. Telling lies is a normal stage of development which children usually grow out of. For some it is a sign of a more serious emotional problem. When dealing with lies, feed back to the child that their behaviour is unacceptable, without being too punitive, and encourage them to deal with the situation in a more mature and honest fashion.

Helping children to understand and cope with their feelings

Children experience their emotions intensely, and at times may become overwhelmed. The role of the parent or staff member is to help children to understand and to talk about their feelings rather than to act on them (often in the form of misbehaviour).

In the playground, children have to manage challenging situations, particularly when they are learning to get on with others. They will experience a range of emotions including anger, elation, excitement, frustration and distress. In such situations, rather than giving advice or telling children what to do, try to demonstrate understanding.

If a child is showing anger, you may find yourself tempted to say something like 'Calm down and stop being so silly'. Alternatively, you could try putting into words the emotion that the child is experiencing. For example:

'I can see that you are angry, but shouting like that won't help to change your friend's mind'. Or, when a child is distressed by losing a game, rather than saying: 'Never mind, you will win next time', you could say: 'I know it can be upsetting to lose; most people feel disappointed when it happens'. This can have a surprisingly calming effect.

There are many other ways in which LTSs can help children to manage their feelings – see the case study below.

> During a training session a team of LTSs described how they made a special arrangement with a year 5 pupil who was finding it difficult to control his temper. Whenever he felt he was about 'to blow' he would find an LTS who would give him a few minutes to help him to calm down.

Another way to help children to understand the language of feelings is to describe how children's behaviour is affecting you. For example, you can say something like: 'When you turn your back on me, I feel really fed up'. This is an example of demonstrating to the children how *you* would like *them* to express themselves.

Touching

Many LTSs describe how they touch children as a way of showing affection and to build relationships. This needs to be done carefully, and will be discussed further in Chapter 10.

Offering praise and showing children that you have confidence in them

Children crave attention, and so commenting on and praising behaviour is likely to build their self-esteem as well as improve their behaviour. Descriptive praise involves commenting on the behaviour that you like in some detail. Rather than saying 'Good boy' when a child shares equipment, try saying something like 'I am really pleased with the way you shared your game with Simon. It's made him much happier'. This sort of praise has much more meaning and impact.

ACTIVITY 3

Practise giving descriptive praise to your team colleagues. Offer them details about what you particularly like. It could be about what they have done, what they are wearing, or anything else you are comfortable with commenting on.

With older children in particular, you can show that you have confidence in their ability to sort out their own disputes and arguments. Rather than feeling that you have to solve every disagreement, it may be helpful to ask the involved children what *they* could do to sort out their difficulties. You can also demonstrate your confidence in children's ability by requesting help with tasks and initiatives and seeking their opinions.

Appearing and sounding positive

In the light of the stresses of your job you cannot always look friendly and relaxed. You do, though, want to give the message that you are caring and approachable. In everyday life people can sometimes be unaware of the way we appear to others. We communicate a great deal by our body language, which includes the way we look, how we use our face, our eyes, our hand movements, gestures and the way we hold our bodies.

> In a training session one LTS described how she had a tendency to look grumpy or fierce even when she didn't mean to. She realised that she rarely smiled and often frowned when she felt worried or when she couldn't understand what a child was telling her. This helped her to understand why the younger children in particular often appeared cautious and uncomfortable in her presence.

LTSs describe how there is often an element of acting required in their work. Although children are likely to know if you are being insincere, learning to communicate positively is an important skill to develop.

Your tone of voice and use of words

Your tone of voice matters. LTSs describe how they try to speak in a warm, open tone. It can also help to lower your pitch and to speak slowly and clearly. You will need to ensure that the children understand what you are saying, and that you are using words that are appropriate to the child's age and understanding.

ACTIVITY 4

How do you appear and sound when communicating with children?

Do you often:

● Smile?

● Frown?

● Maintain 'friendly, interested' eye contact?

- Glare?
- Nod your head in an encouraging way when listening?
- Use your hands when you are angry?
- Point your finger, clench your fists, stab the air or fold your arms in front of your body?
- Shout at the children?

Think about the way you sound when you are angry. Is your tone calm and firm, or do you become high pitched? How quickly do you speak?

Ask a trusted colleague for some feedback about the above points. You may not agree with their feedback, but at least you have a chance to learn about yourself.

Listening

Listening to children is one of the most important ways to build positive relationships with children. Many adults have a tendency to ignore, contradict or rush children when they are talking. We may also finish their sentences, or tell them what they are thinking or feeling. At times it can be difficult to give them the attention they deserve as different groups of children are demanding your attention at the same time, or you are called away mid-discussion to deal with an accident or a fight. Many LTSs describe how they make a considerable effort to find the time to listen when they feel there is an issue of importance.

ACTIVITY 5

Think of reasons why it is important to listen to children.

1
2
3
4
5

Your list may include some of the following:

- Listening helps to build good relationships.
- We all need to be listened to as it helps us to feel valued, respected and cared for.
- Children's self-esteem will suffer if they are not listened to.
- Listening helps us to understand 'what happened'.
- It helps children to feel we are being fair.
- Children often have important things to say.
- We may hear about serious problems including child abuse or bullying.
- We want to encourage children to express themselves.

Active listening

Listening is a skilled activity which involves:

- Looking interested
- Hearing what is said
- Remembering what has been said
- Checking out you understand what is being said
- Trying not to interrupt until the child has said what they need to say

(Adapted from Burnham and Jones 2002)

Open and closed questions

When a child is telling you something, you want to understand as fully as possible what they are trying to communicate. One way to do this is by asking an open question. This is a question that encourages the person to describe in their own words what they think or feel. When asking open questions, you can use words like 'Tell me about', 'Why', 'How' and 'What'.

Example

If a child says: 'I hate school', and looks distressed, hopefully you will find the time to understand what is upsetting her, by asking an open question. You may say:

Why do you hate school?

What do you hate about school?

What happened at school?

You will then need to listen carefully to the child's response and if still unclear, ask another open question.

A closed response to the same statement 'I hate school' would be:

Is it because your best friend is away?

Is it because the work is too hard?

Of course you like school. Aren't they the best days of your life?

In response, you are likely to get a yes or no answer, which is not very useful. It is helpful to practise asking open questions.

ACTIVITY 6

These are all closed questions. Can you rephrase them as open questions?

1 Was your test hard?
2 Is your teacher cross?
3 Do you hate PE?
4 Did she hit you?
5 Are you feeling upset?

No matter how well you try to understand what is happening to a child, they may not want to talk. We cannot make children tell us what is on their mind, but we can use a range of skills to encourage them. When a child is reluctant to communicate, you can try:

- Asking a different open question.
- Changing the subject and returning to the problem later.
- Asking the child if there is anyone else they would like to talk to. This is not a failure, as we all find different people easier to talk to at different times.
- Suggesting that you are available at a later time if the child wishes to talk to you.

You may need to report your concerns to the class teacher.

Listening to both sides of the story

When children are in dispute, it is important that you are seen to be fair by listening carefully to both sides of the story. Try asking each child (or group of children) to take turns to say what happened, and listen to each other without interruption. Remove the audience of onlookers, and allow the children involved in the incident to calm down if necessary. You can also summarise what you have heard and encourage the children to come to their own solutions whenever possible. If you need to take action, explain clearly to them what you are going to do, and why you are doing it.

Responding sensitively to what you hear

As well as listening carefully you will also need to consider carefully how to respond to what you have been told or asked.

When children talk about difficult issues

Children can be extremely open about their life and may choose to tell you personal and at times shocking information. There is no easy way to respond to a child's pain.

An LTS described her horror when an infant child told her 'out of the blue' that he was upset because his baby sister had died. She described how she became confused and speechless.

ACTIVITY 7

Think about how you would respond to a year 4 child who tells you that their:

1 Mum is very ill.
2 Dad has left home.
3 Grandmother has just died.
4 Dad has a new girlfriend or boyfriend.

In such situations, LTSs often describe desperately wanting to make the child feel better. Some describe the temptation of telling the child 'I'm sure Mum will get better' or 'Dad will come back home soon'. It is unhelpful to falsely reassure children by promising happy endings. You also need to avoid asking too many questions as this can make you appear to be nosy.

The safest way to respond is to ask the child how they are feeling and to be sensitive to their response. The child has chosen to tell you their story for a reason, and if they do not want to talk about it, they'll let you know. If you are uncomfortable in this role, find someone else for the child to talk to and remember to inform the class teacher of issues of importance.

Answering children's questions

As a trusted adult you will be asked questions about a range of issues. When giving answers you will need to take into account the child's age and understanding as well as their possible reason for the query. Questions about death, sex, religion, illness, may be difficult to answer, so before answering, consider your response carefully. You may decide to refer the child to another member of staff.

When children ask complex questions, for example 'Why do mummies get so upset?', rather than answering the question directly, you may need to understand what the child is trying to make sense of. If you feel uncomfortable about discussing such personal issues, you can suggest that the child talks to their teacher.

Confidentiality

When you build positive relationships with children and listen well, they are likely to confide in you. You are required to tell an appropriate member of staff if you are worried about incidents of child abuse, bullying, racism, family problems, emotional distress or any other issues that concern you. Children will need to know that you will not gossip about them or share their confidences inappropriately.

This subject will be discussed further in Chapters 6 and 10.

Being consistent, firm and fair

Lunchtime supervisors often describe the importance of having fun with children but also knowing when to draw the line and become firm when necessary. The need to be consistent and fair has already been discussed and these subjects will be revisited in Chapters 4 and 5.

Being a positive role model

It is easy to underestimate how important you can be to the children you work with. If you are good to them, you will be viewed as a positive adult to learn from and to model themselves on. Male LTSs have a valuable role, as they can show children an example of a caring man. Older LTSs can have a special 'grandparent' role and supervisors from ethnic minority groups will offer children the chance to relate to people from other cultures.

Children learn from what we do, more than from what we say. LTSs often describe how children notice every detail, including their moods, their hairstyles, their behaviour or their clothes. By observing, children are making sense of the way people behave and what it is like to be an adult who may be very different from those in their own family.

If you want children to be well behaved and respectful you will need to be well behaved towards them and show them respect. If you present as a genuine and honest person, who is not afraid to apologise for mistakes, the children will learn how to conduct themselves in a similar way. This will provide them with a positive role model.

ACTIVITY 8

Being a positive role model brings with it a range of responsibilities.

Think of how you demonstrate to children (by the way you behave) how they can behave towards others.

1

2

3

4

5

6

Your answers may include:

● Being polite
● Being respectful in the way you talk to children
● Being fair, and listening to both sides
● Being open and friendly
● Being encouraging and accepting
● Explaining why you want things done
● Talking about your own feelings when appropriate
● Being honest, and saying when you don't know something
● Apologising when you make mistakes

Factors that interfere with building positive relationships with children

Communicating with children who do not speak English

There are various ways to develop relationships with children who do not speak English. These include the use of non-verbal communication like miming, smiling and appropriate touch. You can also play games and use songs and rhymes. Give instructions by offering practical examples in simple language. Using another LTS or child to act as an interpreter can be constructive, as long as they are willing to help. Children in this situation often learn to speak English at an impressive rate.

Children whom you struggle to relate to

No matter how hard you try, or how skilled you may be, there are likely to be children whom you find difficult to relate to. This may be the result of a personality clash, or a range of difficulties experienced by you or the child. If you are experiencing a personality clash, ask yourself what in particular you find difficult about the child or who do they remind you of.

It may help to know that if you are feeling like this, there is a good chance that other adults are experiencing similar emotions. Try not to take such 'failures' personally. Relationships with children will have their ups and downs, and progress will often come in small changes.

What happens when relationships go wrong?

When you have worked really hard to build a relationship with a child, you may feel desperately disappointed when things go wrong. This is not unusual, as children, and indeed adults, will resort to old ways at times of pressure or crisis. Try not to take this too personally, and to rebuild the relationship. Progress with troubled children comes in very small changes, and everyone will have off-days. Strategies to rebuild relationships with children will be explored in Chapter 4.

Conclusion

In this chapter many of the necessary skills to develop relationships have been explored, and some of the potential difficulties have been outlined. Human relationships are complex, and there will be no easy formula or 'magic wand' to wave to guarantee success. There is always more to learn and we constantly develop by watching others, by talking to colleagues, and by thinking about how our actions can be improved. Children will forgive us if we occasionally get things wrong, as long as we show them that we are trying our best and that we are committed to their well-being.

CHAPTER 4

Encouraging positive behaviour in the playground and in the dining room

Introduction

LTSs are responsible for managing behaviour and keeping children safe. It is easy to underestimate how difficult this can be. After a structured morning in the classroom, young children appear to be programmed to run, shout, climb (anything there is to be climbed including the spiked fence), splash in puddles, kick anything that can be kicked, and throw objects no matter what the shape or size. You will often be required to stop them doing what they particularly enjoy and in this the seeds of conflict can be sown.

In the past, misbehaviour was dealt with by threat of, or by the use of, physical punishment and humiliation. In schools today we try to understand why children misbehave, and to help them to learn the consequences of their actions. We also encourage them to become well-balanced, self disciplined human beings. Effective behaviour management depends on having skilled staff working together, using a range of agreed strategies, in a well-organised environment.

There is never a single correct way to manage behaviour, as every school and child will be different and every adult will have their own unique way of doing things. There are, however, methods which can be particularly effective. This chapter starts by exploring the reasons why children misbehave. It will then summarise some of the theories that have influenced behaviour management, and will outline a range of ways to encourage children to behave positively.

Why children misbehave

When considering how best to encourage children to behave, it is helpful to have some understanding of the reasons underlying their misbehaviour.

ACTIVITY 1

In groups, write down a quick list of reasons explaining why children misbehave. Compare your list with your colleagues'.

Reasons for misbehaviour may include the child:

- Being unmotivated due to low self-esteem
- Experiencing family problems/crises
- Being the subject of abuse or harsh parenting
- Reacting to peer pressure or bullying
- Reacting to the 'high' or 'low' expectations of others
- Finding the work too difficult or too easy
- Being unwell, hungry, thirsty, hot, tired, over-excited or responding to 'raging hormones'
- Being from a different culture, with language difficulties or different expectations
- Experiencing special educational needs, disability or medical problems
- 'Testing' to see how far they can go
- Attention seeking – or bidding for power
- Reacting to unclear or inconsistent rules and expectations
- Responding to poor teaching
- Reacting to pressures due to school tests, for example SATs

The following case studies demonstrate reasons for misbehaviour, and show how the LTSs' understanding helped.

CASE STUDY 1

A child displayed disobedient behaviour following the death of a close family member. Once the LTSs understood this, they were more able to respond to her in a caring rather than punitive way.

CASE STUDY 2

A child became agitated when the LTS insisted that he look at her when she was talking. The LTS remembered that in certain cultures direct eye contact can be seen as confrontational, and was able to amend her request.

CASE STUDY 3

An LTS became aware that a junior school child would not do as she asked when with her friends. The LTS was aware of the power of peer pressure and decided to remove the audience of children.

ACTIVITY 2

Think of examples of some of the factors that you have taken into account when managing children's behaviour.

How have you adapted your interventions in the light of these factors?

A theory to explain children's misbehaviour

Redolf Dreikurs, a psychologist, maintained that children misbehave as an unhelpful way to try to meet their needs and to find acceptance within the family or group. He described how misbehaviour is often based on their mistaken beliefs about themselves and others. When dealing with this we need to help children to understand their behaviour, and find better ways to meet their needs. Dreikurs *et al.* (1998) described four categories of children who misbehave.

Attention seekers

Some children have learnt that if they misbehave they will be given lots of attention, which they possibly fail to get in other areas of their life. Dreikurs believed that 90 per cent of all misbehaviour is to gain attention. In response, many schools try to reward positive behaviour and whenever possible to remove attention from the negative behaviour.

Power seekers

Such children appear to need to have the last word, to dominate and to win. When working with them, you are likely to feel challenged or threatened, with the desire to 'make them do as they are told'. The misbehaviour is likely to continue when the child is challenged. This group also plays to an audience. In response, you will need to find ways to defuse the power battle. Such strategies will be discussed later in Chapter 5.

Revenge seekers

This group of children believe that they have been badly treated in life and so attempt to get their own back on others. The target of the revenge may be teachers, LTSs or other children, and sometimes this can result in bullying behaviour. Ways to help these children are outlined in Chapter 6, which tackles bullying.

Children who feel inadequate

These children have become discouraged and have given up. They believe they are not as good as others and have no chance of succeeding or belonging, so fail to join in to avoid further humiliation or embarrassment. Such children can be difficult to engage with and are unlikely to ask for help. Strategies of praise and reward can be helpful.

ACTIVITY 3

Can you think of children with whom you work who fit into the above groups?

When dealing with their behaviour, what has worked?

Can you think of occasions when you have helped children to understand their behaviour, and to think about how they could do things differently?

Theories that have influenced the way schools manage children's behaviour

Here are some of the most popular theories that have influenced the way schools manage behaviour.

Behaviourist Theory (B.F. Skinner)

B.F. Skinner in the 1940s described how animals and humans learn to repeat behaviour which leads to pleasure, and to avoid behaviour which results in pain. When given praise or attention for certain behaviours, children are therefore likely to repeat this behaviour, as praise and attention are pleasurable. Giving such praise is known as positive reinforcement. Punishment is unpleasant and so it is likely that behaviour that is punished will decrease.

Social Learning Theory (Albert Bandura)

Social learning focuses on how learning occurs in a social situation, when we observe others and model ourselves upon them in an attempt to gain reward, praise, acceptance or pleasure. Children therefore need to be given lots of opportunities to see others being successful, and to be encouraged to believe that they can be successful too. The social learning theorists outline the importance of peer pressure, and the powerful effect of positive role models (Ormrod 1999).

Self-Fulfilling Prophecy and Labelling Theory (Merton, Rosenthal and Becker)

This theory suggests that children will be influenced by the way in which others view them. Children want approval, so when we communicate the belief that they are good, the child is likely to believe in themselves and to behave in a desirable way. If we communicate the belief that they are bad or naughty, the child is likely to see themselves as bad and live up to these expectations. In such circumstances children are being labelled good or bad, and these labels are likely to stick and to become self-fulfilling prophecies. For example, 'I believe I am bad and so I will behave in a bad way. I will then be told I am bad'. Ways to avoid this vicious circle will be discussed later in the chapter.

The Rights and Responsibility Model – the four Rs (Bill Rogers)

Bill Rogers proposes a four Rs model which is popular in schools today. He describes how using the ideas of 'rights, responsibilities, rules and routines' can help to manage behaviour.

- All pupils have the *right* to feel safe in school, the *right* to learn, and the *right* to be treated with respect and dignity. These rights need to be balanced with responsibilities.
- All pupils are *responsible* for letting others learn.
- Schools need clear *rules* and consequences to protect the rights of others. For example, 'If you disrupt the lesson you are interfering with other people's right to learn, and so you will miss playtime'.
- Routines are the way schools organise things, for example how children are expected to line up in the dining room.

Bill Rogers outlines a range of strategies to encourage acceptable behaviour based on communicating clear expectations. He also describes how we can manage behaviour in a way that keeps conflict to the minimum. This will be discussed below and in Chapter 5.

Culturally Sensitive Behaviour Management (Lalit Kumar 1991)

This theory outlines the importance of understanding how social ideas, values and standards of behaviour may differ depending on a person's culture. Behaviour that we do not initially understand, and which we may see as problematic, is more likely to make sense when viewed in its cultural context. For example, in some societies males are unwilling to recognise female authority. This may explain why some male children obviously ignore requests made by female LTSs.

Lalit Kumar describes how, when working in a multicultural community, to avoid miscommunication, schools need to understand the specific meaning of children's body language and non-verbal communication. The use of eye contact is an interesting example. In Western society we see the lack of eye contact as a sign of rudeness, whilst Asian or Japanese pupils may look away from adults as a sign of respect. Black Caribbean pupils are more likely to see prolonged eye contact as confrontational. Hand gestures and facial expressions are also easy to misunderstand. For example, in some cultures people tend to smile or laugh when under pressure, which may be mistakenly viewed as rudeness rather than anxiety.

Ways to encourage children's positive behaviour – a whole school model

There are many other important ways to encourage children to behave positively. These include all school staff including LTSs:

- Being firm, fair and consistent
- Having high expectations for all pupils
- Focusing on what you would like children to do, rather than what you would not like them to do
- Planning for good behaviour
- Offering children praise and reward
- Separating and responding to a child's behaviour without condemning the child
- Using your understanding of why children misbehave (see case studies on page 34)
- Encouraging children to take responsibility for their own behaviour
- Being an effective role model
- Considering the importance of physical and environmental issues

Each of these points will be discussed below.

Being firm, fair and consistent

When staff members work together in a firm, fair and consistent way, children are more likely to behave well. They will feel secure, and clear about your expectations. They will also be unable to play one team member off against another, or LTSs off against teaching staff. This is known as a whole school approach to behaviour management. To achieve consistency, schools will require clear channels of communication and a strong, well-written behaviour policy. This is outlined in greater detail in Chapter 5 and in the Notes for managers for this chapter.

LTSs will also need to demonstrate to children that they are prepared to do what they say; avoid making promises they can't keep; be fair and listen to both sides of the story; offer explanations for their requests; and adapt their decisions when appropriate.

Have high expectations for all pupils

LTSs should have high expectations of all pupils and communicate these clearly. To do this assertively you will need to develop a sense of authority, which often comes from a belief in our own abilities. Without having to shout, nag or threaten, you can learn to convey the message 'This is what I expect, and I have no doubt that you will do it'.

Ways to communicate your expectations

LTSs describe a range of ways in which they communicate their expectations without resorting to shouting. Many believe shouting at children is counter-productive, and that everyone just gets louder. By shouting you also risk frightening small children, or losing their respect.

Having a range of agreed non-verbal signals

LTSs may use a range of agreed non-verbal signals to communicate their expectations to children. These often involve the use of hand gestures, which children may be required to copy. For example, rather than shouting, you may use this method to signal that you want quiet in the dining room. This is most effective when the whole school community use the same signals to communicate their expectations, and when it is consistently reinforced.

ACTIVITY 4

In small groups think of someone at work who clearly communicates their high expectations in relation to children's behaviour.

Describe how they do this, considering their body language, their tone of voice and any other relevant factors.

Some of your answers may include:

- The person's body language backs up the words they use. For example, they stand 'tall and firm' when giving an instruction.
- They appear to mean what they say, and expect others to cooperate.
- Their tone of voice is clear, low and firm.
- They use words which are understood by the children.
- Their sentences are short and to the point.
- They speak slowly and pause, repeating instructions when necessary.
- They give clear instructions about what they want to happen, rather than what they don't want to happen.

The person you have selected may be a teacher or senior manager, and although their status automatically gives them greater authority, you too can learn to communicate in this way.

The use of body language, facial expressions and tone of voice has already been discussed in Chapter 3. Without having to say a word, LTSs describe how they can communicate approval or disapproval by just looking. This has been playfully named 'the look', and in a training session an LTS amused the group by describing how a small child asked her 'Why are you telling me off with your eyes?'

When considering your voice, bear in mind that it can help to lower it and slow down the pace when you are aiming to give instructions. You may also need to speak fairly loudly, without shouting. By using fewer words, with pauses, you can actually help to keep the child's attention. Similarly, repeating the main part of your instruction slowly and clearly may help to show that you mean what you say. This is known as assertive communication.

ACTIVITY 5

Act out how you could assertively ask a group of children to stop playing and to line up for dinner. Think about your use of words, tone of voice, how quickly you speak, the number of times you paused, or repeated the instruction. Also think about your body language and facial expression. If possible do this with a partner and give each other feedback about what was done well and what could be improved.

It also makes all the difference when your authority is backed by other staff members. This has been explored in Chapter 1 and in Notes for managers on page 100.

Focus on what you would like children to do, rather than what you would like them not to do

When managing behaviour we often say things like 'Don't run' or 'Don't forget'. The use of too many don'ts can sound 'naggy' and tends to switch children off. For example, a child may be holding their dinner tray with one hand and tipping it dangerously. You are concerned that they are going to drop the food so respond by shouting 'Don't drop it'. Alternatively, you could say, 'Hold the tray carefully'. Although this is a little clearer, it assumes that the child's understanding of the words 'Hold it carefully' is the same as yours. Children are most likely to do as asked if we describe in detail what we would like them to do. For example, in the above incident you could say, 'Hold your tray with two hands and make sure it is straight'. This leaves little doubt about what is being requested.

ACTIVITY 6

Fill in Column 3 with a description of what you could say to a child to explain what you would like them to do. The first example has been filled in to help you.

The behaviour	Your usual response	Description of what you want to happen
A child is balancing dangerously on a climbing frame.	Be careful. You'll fall…	I want to see both feet on the bar please, and hold on with both hands

A child is walking towards the road.	Don't go in the road...
A child is shouting when telling you what happened.	Stop shouting please...
A child is bossing the others around.	Don't be so bossy...
A child is about to drop their cup.	Don't drop it...

Possible answers:

Stay on the pavement.

Speak quietly please.

Try to take turns to decide.

Hold your cup with two hands please.

Planning for good behaviour

Effective management of behaviour involves planning for good behaviour rather than reacting when things go wrong. This involves thinking about the potential behavioural problems at lunchtime, and planning to avoid them. For example, you may know which children wind each other up in the dining room, and so you can ensure they do not sit together. You may notice that playground behaviour becomes particularly difficult 15 minutes before the end of the lunch hour, when large numbers of children are out in the playground, and so you can decide to introduce a period of structured games to re-focus their energy. Your team will need time to plan together how best to achieve these improvements and to discuss them with your line manager. Planning for good behaviour can also include being positive, giving lots of praise, and thinking about ways to avoid confrontation. These will be explored in greater detail below, and in the next chapter.

ACTIVITY 7

Can you think of other examples of how you have anticipated difficulties and planned to avoid them?

Offering praise and reward

Some theorists suggest that we need to praise children at least six times more than we tell them off, as giving attention to behaviour (either good or bad) will result in it being repeated. The praise offered needs to be genuine; otherwise children will sense your insincerity. The value of offering descriptive praise has been discussed in the previous chapter.

Catch them being good

Even when children have a tendency to regularly misbehave a lot of the time, it is helpful to 'catch them being good', and to praise them for it. This is demonstrated by the case study below.

> An LTS described a particularly disruptive boy in year 5 who had family problems. He seemed to thrive on being told off, as a way to get himself noticed. The LTS struggled to find behaviour to praise, but along with teaching staff made a decision to focus on even the smallest piece of positive behaviour. They decided to praise him when he queued up quietly for lunch or shared playground equipment with others. With time, positive behaviour became more frequent and their relationships gradually improved.

Systems schools create to reward positive behaviour

Schools often have systems which use this principle. For example, staff may be encouraged to comment on the children who *are* lining up well or putting away their playground equipment, rather than focusing on the children who *are not*. A smile or a thumbs up as well as verbal praise can work wonders, particularly with younger children who often join in with the desired behaviour to earn your approval.

Schools may also introduce rewards systems where stickers, house points or certificates are given at lunchtime, as well as during the day, for good behaviour or effort. A 'table of the week' may be created, where the best-behaved group of children sit at a decorated table at lunchtime, and are awarded extra privileges. These systems need to be linked with the whole school behaviour policy and reviewed regularly. Many LTSs believe these schemes can be extremely helpful, although some find them difficult to implement fairly. There is often a concern that the quiet, well-behaved children tend to be overlooked.

ACTIVITY 8

Think of the times you have encouraged good behaviour by giving children praise or reward. What sorts of behaviour do you praise?

Observe your practice over the next few days. How often do you offer praise and how often do you tell children off? Are you happy with this balance?

Can you think of times when you have given pupils' unacceptable behaviour lots of attention?

> What systems do you have at lunchtime to reward positive behaviour?
>
> What could improve these systems?

Separate and respond to a child's behaviour without condemning the child

As already outlined in this chapter, if we label children, it is likely to affect the way they feel and behave. Even as adults we often can remember the labels we were given as children. When correcting children, it is more helpful to comment on the behaviour we wish to change. For example, if a child hurts another you can say, 'That was an unkind thing *to do*' rather than 'You are an unkind girl'. By focusing on the behaviour, you are less likely to damage the child's self-esteem, and will give the message that a child can behave differently next time. Children are very quick to imitate adults and to label each other. This behaviour needs to be challenged too.

ACTIVITY 9

Can you remember the labels you were given as a child?

How do you think these labels have affected you in adult life?

Encouraging children to take responsibility for their own behaviour

Ways you can do this include:

- Involving them in drawing up playground and dining room rules.
- Requesting feedback about how they experience the rules at lunchtime and encouraging suggestions for improvements.
- Discussing behaviour issues with children whenever possible. It is sometimes helpful to ask a child what they would do if they were you.
- Teaching children basic conflict resolution skills by encouraging them to discuss their difficulties and come to their own solutions. This has been discussed further in Chapter 3.
- Encouraging them to become involved with lunchtime schemes and initiatives.

Being an effective role model

As discussed in Chapter 3, the way you behave at work will demonstrate to children how you expect them to behave. They will learn a great deal by seeing how you act towards them and others. Some of the important qualities to model include calmness, predictability, politeness, tolerance, listening skills and how to resolve conflict.

Considering the importance of physical and environmental issues

Many physical and environmental factors will affect children's behaviour. LTSs describe how on windy days all hell is likely to let loose. If children are bored, hungry, thirsty, hot and bothered, full of food additives or uncomfortable, tempers are more likely to flare.

If the dining room is unattractive, very noisy, and the queues are long, behaviour is likely to deteriorate. The state of the toilets is important, as research suggests that large numbers of children will refuse to use them if they are dirty or smelly, and so may spend their day in discomfort.

Schools respond to these difficulties by providing breakfast clubs and working water fountains, pagodas or other shade giving constructions in the playground. There is not a lot you can do about windy days!

The organisation of the dining room will contribute to children's positive or negative behaviour.

A dining room checklist

In your school...	Yes	No
is the dining room well decorated and attractive?	☐	☐
is the noise level in the dining room acceptable?	☐	☐
would you like to eat in this environment?	☐	☐
are the dining room rules and routines clear and on display?	☐	☐
are children required to wait in queues for an unacceptable amount of time? If not, what can be changed?	☐	☐
do you have systems to gain children's attention and reduce the noise without having to resort to shouting?	☐	☐
are children encouraged to develop acceptable table manners?	☐	☐

Although the responsibility for making major changes rests with senior managers and governors, you can observe things and feed back your concerns and ideas for improvement, as well as changing some things yourself.

Conclusion

If you are able to successfully encourage children to behave well, you are less likely to have to deal with difficult and challenging incidents. A number of strategies and skills have been outlined above. In the next chapter, ways to deal with unacceptable behaviour will be explored.

CHAPTER 5

Managing unacceptable behaviour at lunchtime

Introduction

Dealing with unacceptable behaviour is often the area that LTSs are most keen to discuss. Perhaps they secretly hope they will learn the magic answers to achieve a perfect lunchtime full of well-behaved children. Unfortunately, these answers do not exist, and perfectly behaved children do not exist either. However, there are skills, strategies and whole school practices that can help you.

This chapter starts by exploring a whole school model of behaviour management. Effective strategies to deal with unacceptable behaviour will then be examined. The chapter concludes by focusing on dealing with challenges including verbal abuse and violence.

Managing unacceptable behaviour, a whole school model

Challenging and correcting behaviour (just like encouraging acceptable behaviour) needs to happen in line with the school's behaviour policy. This is an important document which outlines the school's philosophy, expectations, rules and sanctions (punishments) relevant to behaviour during all parts of the school day.

Having clear and consistent consequences in response to misbehaviour

Your school will need to agree on consequences for unacceptable behaviour. Sanctions may include time out, the loss of privileges, being reported verbally or in writing, or for more serious incidents, being sent to a senior manager to be dealt with. These sanctions should be implemented consistently at playtime, lunchtime and during the rest of the school day. Agreement is needed among the whole staff team about:

- What type of behaviour warrants particular sanctions
- When behaviour must be reported, and how this is to be done
- How many warnings the child should be given before action is taken
- How long the punishment should last
- What will happen next if the behaviour does not improve
- Who will follow up on reported incidents
- How you can obtain feedback on how reported incidents have been dealt with

The use of 'time out' as a sanction

Many schools have special places in the playground (often a bench or a wall) where children can be sent to for a few minutes to calm down and to 'think about their behaviour'. This cooling off period also removes the child from a difficult situation. There may be a supervised indoor place within the school, where children can be sent as a punishment for more serious offences. As already discussed, it is important when using sanctions to keep the focus on the child's behaviour and to remind them that you expect better of them in the future.

Strategies for challenging unacceptable behaviour

This section will focus on skills and strategies which individuals and teams can use to challenge unacceptable behaviour. There is no easy way to make children behave. What works for one person may not work for another and what works on one day may not work the next. Successful behaviour management is like having a bag of tricks, and knowing how to select the most effective one for a particular situation.

Behaviour that particularly winds you up

Managing children's behaviour can stir up powerful feelings. We are all likely to find some behaviour difficult to cope with, and it is not unusual for children to sense our weak spots, and to push them to the limit. Knowing what winds you up, and if possible why it does so, may help you to react in a calmer and less emotional way.

ACTIVITY 1

Discuss:

What behaviour really 'gets you going'?

How does it make you feel?

What would you *like* to say or do to the child responsible for the behaviour?

The behaviour usually listed includes:

- Rudeness/attitude
- Swearing
- Violence
- Bullying
- Being ignored
- Children making rude faces, mimicking you or giggling behind your back

When dealing with unacceptable behaviour, you will need to make decisions about when and how best to challenge the child.

Types of challenges

Challenging children's behaviour respectfully can help them to learn what is socially acceptable. Being harsh or aggressive can be counter-productive and may distress sensitive or younger children. Types of challenges include:

Explaining what you would like to happen, and why

For example, a child splashes in a puddle in the playground, and you may say, 'I would like you to move away from the puddle or you will get wet and have to sit in wet clothes all afternoon'. This informs the child what you would like to happen and what the consequences will be if the behaviour continues. It is not unusual to have to repeat such requests on many occasions.

The use of warnings and consequences

If your request for change has been unsuccessful, you may decide to introduce a warning and a consequence. The warning acts to give the child a choice. For example, 'If you don't stop splashing, I will have to report you'. If the child does not do as instructed, you will need to follow through with your threat and report him.

Firm challenges when there is violence or danger

When responding to violence or danger, you will need to challenge a child assertively, often without giving an explanation. For example, if she is climbing onto the roof, you are likely to say in a firm, calm and strong voice: 'Get down now' and to discuss the reasons when the child is safely on the ground.

The 'broken record'

This type of challenge can be used when you have already given an explanation for your instruction. For example, you have asked a child to come off the climbing frame, and have explained why. She refuses and starts to argue, so you repeat the statement a number of times in calm and firm manner (as if the record has got stuck): 'I want you to get down now'. The child will know by your tone and by the repetition of the instruction that you are not going to change your mind. If this is not working, you will need to try another method, possibly a warning followed by a consequence.

Strategies you can use to reduce the risk of confrontation

Bill Rogers describes the importance of managing behaviour in a way that keeps power struggles and confrontation to the minimum.

Some of his strategies include:

- Responding to incidents that matter
- Keeping the focus on the primary behaviour
- Tactical ignoring
- Partial agreement
- Distraction
- Using the language of choice

These will now be discussed.

Responding to incidents that matter

When managing behaviour, it is important to know when to decide to let things go. In other words it helps to pick your battles. This is not a case of being too lazy to tackle difficulties, but more a case of deciding what matters and dealing with it consistently and effectively. For example, if a child makes a silly face behind your back; you may decide to let this go. This is known as *tactical ignoring*. You should never ignore behaviour which is violent, unsafe, racist, seriously insulting to you or to others.

Keeping the focus on the primary behaviour

You see a child throwing earth at another child in the playground. You challenge her firmly and she responds in an angry way: 'Why are you picking on me? I wasn't the only one throwing earth. It's not fair'. In this situation the throwing of the earth is the *primary* behaviour and the child's angry response when challenged is the *secondary* behaviour, which is her way of defending herself, appearing cool in front of friends, or distracting you. Secondary behaviour can also take the form of being rude, aggressive body language, or having the clever last word. Rather than going into attack and engaging in a power struggle with the child, it is far more useful to keep the focus on the primary behaviour (your initial challenge about throwing earth) by saying something like:

'Maybe you weren't the only one throwing earth, but I saw you throw it and I want you to stop now and move away from the grass.'

If the child answers back rudely, rather than getting sucked into a full-scale argument, continue to comment on the earth throwing and what you would like to happen.

Tactical ignoring

As described above, tactical ignoring involves a decision to ignore behaviour for a particular reason. For example, a child may be messing around in the queue, knowing that this is a great way to get your attention. You make a decision to ignore him completely, and to focus your attention on the children on either side who are standing quietly. It would be inappropriate to ignore safety issues, aggression, violence, bullying or serious incidents.

Partial agreement

In the above earth throwing incident, the response given to the child included the words 'Maybe you weren't the only one throwing earth, but…'. This is an example of a *partial agreement*. By agreeing with some of what the child has said, you are showing that you are prepared to meet them halfway. This can have a calming effect, which then allows you both to focus on the original behaviour.

Distraction

In some situations you may decide to distract a child who is misbehaving. For example, when a child is making rude faces behind your back, you may decide to ignore this and to distract her by encouraging her to help you to collect the playground equipment. By doing so you are refusing to rise to the bait, whilst also engaging her in a constructive activity.

Using the language of choice

Imagine you are in the playground and you see a child drop a piece of litter. When asked, he refuses to pick it up. You are now faced with a decision about how best to gain the pupil's cooperation, without making the situation worse. You may try to appeal to the child's better nature by saying in a friendly way, 'Please help me and pick up the paper', or you might turn it into as game and suggest that you pick it up together. We cannot *make* a child do something that they are refusing to do. Giving them a limited choice can, however, take the heat out of the situation and result in a positive outcome. This is illustrated in the examples below.

CASE STUDY 1

When the child refuses to pick up the litter, you could give him limited choice by saying: 'I do want you to pick up the paper. Would you like to do it now or in one minute?' This gives a child some say in the matter and so they no longer feel 'cornered', or that they have to fight to win. It is amazing how often the child backs down with the sense that they have not lost face.

CASE STUDY 2

A child continues to play with some equipment, when you have told him to put it away. Instead of physically removing it, you could give him a limited choice by saying: 'I want you to put that in the box. Would you like to do it yourself or would you prefer me to do it?' The choice gives the child some control and makes it more likely that he will do as asked.

If the child does not respond, you can give another choice: 'Either you do as I asked or I will have to put your name in the behaviour book. It's up to you.'

In some schools the language of choice is used on an everyday basis as part of the behaviour policy. Staff are encouraged to ask children if they have made 'good' or 'bad' choices, as a way of helping them to consider their actions.

When managing behaviour it is helpful to practise using a range of methods. None of the above will work every time, but if you have a number of options to choose from you are far more likely to be successful.

ACTIVITY 2

How many of the above strategies have you used at work? You may need to remind yourself of these by reading the relevant paragraphs above. Fill in columns 2 and 3.

Type of strategy	Do you use it?	Give an example of how you have used this strategy
	Yes / No	
Challenging with an explanation	☐ / ☐	....
Using a warning followed by a consequence	☐ / ☐	....
Firm challenges when there is violence or danger	☐ / ☐	....
The 'broken record'	☐ / ☐	....
Using the language of choice	☐ / ☐	....
Respond to incidents that matter	☐ / ☐	....
Keep the focus on the primary behaviour	☐ / ☐	....
Tactical ignoring	☐ / ☐	....
Partial agreement	☐ / ☐	....

Consider the behaviour management case studies below. Try to be as flexible as possible and think of a number of ways to deal with each problem.

ACTIVITY 3

Behaviour management case studies:

What strategies would you try in the following situations and why?

1   You see a boy on the flat roof of the school dining hall about to rescue a ball. He refuses to come down when you tell him to.

2   There is commotion on one of the tables in the dining room. When you go over you find that children have been flicking peas at each other. There are eight children on the table. It is not clear how many of them have been involved.

3   When you tell a child to line up she says, 'My mum says you can't make me – you are just the dinner lady.'

4   You see a child drop a wrapper on the floor and ask her to pick it up. She says, 'No – why should I?'

5   There is a puddle in the playground and you explain why they should not get wet. The children continue splashing in it as soon as your back is turned.

6   A group of children call a group of Muslim children racist names.

7   A child, well known for having a short fuse, has lost his temper following an argument with another child. You want him to calm down before discussing his behaviour.

8   You see a group of year 6 children giggle and make faces behind your back.

Coping with the most challenging behaviour

At the start of Chapter 4, the complex reasons for misbehaviour were briefly discussed. For some children, their difficulties may be so great that they regularly resort to unmanageable, violent or extremely abusive behaviour. No matter how expert or skilful you may be, this behaviour is likely to remain problematic. Often these are the children that others are struggling to manage, and it is important not to see their misbehaviour as your personal failure.

Special arrangements that can be helpful

Lunchtime can be a particularly challenging time for some troubled children, and it may help to make special arrangements.

> An LTS described how her school had developed an extremely successful indoor lunchtime club where some of the most troubled children were required to attend on a daily basis. The children were gradually allowed back into the playground on a part-time basis, when they felt able to cope and to behave.

When working with such children, you are likely to need regular backup and support from teaching staff or other involved experts. This may mean that a senior manager joins you in the playground, or that children can be taken into school when necessary.

> At one school the LTSs requested walkie-talkies to be used in emergencies to summon help. Another school developed a red card system where children were given a card to take into the school which signalled the need for immediate backup.

Schools often draw up individual behaviour plans or individual learning plans which outline the school's expectations and targets for particular children to meet. You may find it helpful to meet with the SENCO or class teacher to share relevant information and practice.

Physical contact and restraint

During lunchtime you have a responsibility to keep children safe. However, it is crucial that you do not hurt a child in your attempt to protect others, or when you have lost your temper. The Department for Education and Skills (DfES) produces useful guidelines for staff concerning appropriate physical contact and restraint (for example, Circular 10/98 (DfES 1998a)). Many schools have drawn up their own procedures addressing these issues, including how you are expected to break up fights. You may also be offered specialised training in methods of restraint. Your head teacher is ultimately responsible for how much physical contact support staff use, and so it is important that you receive guidance.

When you have been hurt or verbally abused

Unfortunately, it is not unusual for LTSs to be hit, kicked, and verbally or racially abused by pupils. Such behaviour is unacceptable, and must be taken extremely seriously. On occasions, LTSs have described how they are left feeling stressed, depressed and demoralised. They tend to underplay the incident, believing it to be somehow their fault. Following such attacks, it is important that you feel able to request appropriate help, and that this is made available. This may include seeking an apology from the child, and seeing evidence that the school is taking appropriate action.

Behaving professionally and looking after yourself

Managing challenging behaviour can generate powerful negative feelings. When working with challenging children relationships can be volatile. As the adult you will need to show them that you do not bear a grudge, and that you are ready to rebuild the relationship. You may feel able to apologise if you have lost your temper, or to explain how angry the child's behaviour has made you feel.

> One LTS described an overwhelming desire to hit out at a child who was pushing her to the limit. She resorted to taking a deep breath, and walking away from the situation, leaving a colleague to take over whilst she calmed down.

Others describe counting to ten or removing the child from the situation. Having meetings where you can talk honestly and openly about these pressures can help you behave professionally. You may also find that debriefing and laughing with colleagues at the end of duty can enable you to leave the stresses at the school gate.

Conclusion

During the lunchtime break you have the challenging job of supervising a large number of children in sometimes difficult circumstances. This chapter has offered a range of strategies and whole school practices that will help you to manage children's behaviour. Do not expect to be successful all the time, and try to learn from the times things go wrong, as well as times when things go well.

CHAPTER 6

Dealing with bullying

Introduction

Up to three-quarters of bullying in primary schools is believed to take place in the playground. This makes your role as an LTS crucial in dealing with the problem. This includes identifying, responding to, reporting and recording incidents of bullying. You can also help children to deal with being bullied, and encourage the aggressor to behave more appropriately.

This chapter will start by exploring what constitutes bullying, who is likely to bully or be bullied, and the devastating effects it can have. The chapter will go on to look at what schools can do in response. There are no easy solutions to this problem, but by reading the chapter you will be clearer about the options available to you.

Information about bullying

What is bullying?

Bullying is when people force others, usually smaller people, to do what they want.

Boy, year 5

Bullying is any behaviour which is intended to hurt, threaten or frighten another person or group of people. It is difficult for those being bullied to stop the process. It involves a person or a group of people using their power over others. It can be physical, verbal or emotional.

Pupils' understanding of bullying will vary with age. Infants may confuse bullying with frightening and nasty experiences generally, whilst juniors tend to develop a more mature understanding. Parents also sometimes mistakenly believe that their child is being bullied when they have argued with another child.

Forms of bullying

Young people describe how bullying can take the form of:

- Name calling or teasing
- Being threatened
- Being hit or attacked by being pushed, pulled, pinched or kicked
- Receiving abusive text messages
- Stealing others' possessions
- Being forced to do things
- Being ignored, left out, or isolated by gossip and the spreading of rumours

Who gets bullied?

Some children get bullied because they are somehow different; others are bullied for no obvious reason. Research suggests that the victim may:

- Be gentle, intelligent and creative
- Lack friends
- Be a non-fighter
- Be disabled or have special needs
- Belong to an ethnic minority group, religion or be homosexual
- Be physically different although their physical characteristics may be used as an excuse by the bully
- Behave inappropriately, in a way that annoys or irritates others
- Be someone who shows their feelings
- Often believe that the bullying is their fault
- Keep what's happening secret

Who bullies?

Individuals and groups of boys are most likely to bully others, although girls bully too. Children who bully can come from a range of family backgrounds and social classes. Michelle Elliot describes how some children become 'temporary bullies' in response to a family crisis (for example, the birth of a new baby, or illness in the home). Others bully on a long term regular basis and some describe it as a bad habit they find difficult to break.

Children who bully are likely to:

- Feel insecure and have low self-esteem
- Meet their needs by humiliating or dominating others
- Be scapegoats or victims in their own family
- See feelings and vulnerability as unacceptable weakness
- Lack love and limits
- Have an impulsive temperament

(Summary of Elliot 1994)

The effects of bullying on children

Serious bullying can have an extremely negative impact on a child's self-esteem and quality of life. Damage can be long term and many adults who suffered as children say they have never fully recovered. Victims may develop a range of physical and emotional symptoms. Being bullied may also lead to depression and, in the most serious cases, suicide (Smith 2000).

Michelle Elliot, who founded the anti-bullying organisation Kidscape, describes how victims of bullying may:

- Be unwilling or frightened to go to school
- Begin to underachieve
- Become anxious and withdrawn
- Cry or have nightmares
- Have unexplained bruises or cuts
- Have possessions 'go missing'
- Refuse to say what is wrong
- Start to bully siblings
- Appear unreasonably angry with parents
- Give improbable excuses for any of the above
- Develop physical or emotional symptoms
- Self-harm, attempt or threaten suicide

(Elliot 1994)

What helps children to cope with or avoid being bullied

The three most helpful factors in preventing, or helping pupils to deal with, bullying are: having friends, learning to avoid the bully and learning to stand up for themselves (Thomas Coram Research Unit 2003). Fifteen per cent of the primary school pupils interviewed thought that 'hitting back' would 'always' or 'usually' work to stop bullying. Retaliating with violence is clearly discouraged by schools, but careful use of humour, changing the subject, or walking away from the situation may also be effective

What can schools do?

Develop a clear anti-bullying ethos and anti-bullying policy which is relevant to all members of the school community

Schools can give clear messages that bullying is unacceptable, that immediate action will be taken by all staff, and that children should not suffer in silence. They have a legal duty to draw up procedures to prevent bullying among pupils and to bring these procedures to the attention of staff, parents and pupils.

The role of the LTS in relation to tackling bullying

To work effectively you will need to be able to:

- Identify incidents of bullying
- Make yourself open, accessible and listen to the children
- Use school systems to ensure that information and incidents of bullying are recorded and discussed
- Work with victims of bullying and children who bully, in line with the school anti-bullying policy
- Challenge racist and sexist behaviour
- Encourage bystanders to take action
- Help children to cope with friendship difficulties
- Regularly review playground organisation
- Support existing playground initiatives
- Consult with the children

Identifying and dealing with bullying

In the first part of this chapter some of the key signs and symptoms pointing to the occurrence of bullying were outlined. When looking for bullying you are also keeping an eye on children who look regularly distressed and alone, and on children or groups of children who appear to be dominated or to be dominating others.

It will help to recognise the difference between play fighting and bullying. As research by Peter Smith outlines, children's experience of bullying is often dismissed as 'play fighting' whilst on other occasions staff mistake children's rough-and-tumble play for harmful aggression. Play fighting is extremely common and can help children to acquire skills in relation to assertion and survival. When children are play fighting, you are more likely to see:

smiling or laughing, 'mock' blows or kicks which do not connect or do so only softly, children taking turns at being on top, or chasing the other. By contrast, pupils who are being attacked or physically bullied often frown or look unhappy or angry, try to move away from the aggressor, do not take turns, as the aggressor remains dominant throughout.

(Smith 2000)

Both boys and girls engage in play fighting and in most cases this does not escalate into aggressive fighting. If unclear, ask participants in a friendly tone about what they are doing.

Make yourself open, accessible and listen to children

Ways to develop trusting relationships with children have been explored in Chapter 3, and you may wish to re-read parts of this chapter. Encouraging a child 'to tell' requires an adult's willingness to listen. Victims may be reluctant to tell others about bullying, feeling it is their fault or something they have to deal with alone. Many fear that they will not be believed or that telling adults will make things worse. Children will tell you more when you listen to them in a calm non-judgemental way, and take their concerns seriously. They also need to trust that you will not tell others about the bullying unless necessary. If you will be passing incidents on to others to be dealt with, you should inform the child of this.

In the past, children were discouraged from telling tales, as they were seen to be 'snitching' or 'grassing'. Although you may sometimes feel irritated when children constantly tell on others, try to listen carefully to avoid missing something serious. It helps to find a confidential space away from friends, to talk to children privately. If, having listened, you do not think that the child is being bullied, discuss this with them in a sympathetic way. This leaves the door open for the child to report future incidents if necessary.

Use school systems to ensure that information and incidents of bullying are recorded and discussed

As discussed in previous chapters, sharing information is a two-way process. To be effective, it will help if you know which children are at risk of bullying or being bullied, and who is experiencing serious friendship difficulties or disputes.

Your school will require you to communicate with teaching staff following bullying incidents at lunchtime. When a child is physically injured, you will be required to record it in the incident book, and racist incidents are likely to be recorded in the racial incident book. Verbal bullying, depending on its severity, may be dealt with by you and/or passed on to others.

ACTIVITY 1

How are you informed by other members of staff about who is bullying or who is being bullied?

Are you made aware of children's serious friendship difficulties or group disputes?

Are you clear about your school systems for recording or reporting bullying to the relevant people?

How can communication about bullying in school be improved?

Work with the victim of bullying

Your school's behaviour policy is likely to offer guidance for victims of bullying, including how to be assertive and to report bullying. LTSs can have an important role in helping children to:

- Believe that the bullying is not their fault
- Rebuild their self-esteem
- Develop strategies to cope with bullying, including assertive behaviour
- Know what action is being taken, and by whom

Reassuring children that the bullying is not their fault

No one deserves to be bullied. Children need to be reassured that it is not their fault, and that nothing is terribly wrong with them. They need to know it was right to tell you what happened.

Help to rebuild their self-esteem

By listening, believing and supporting the child, whilst reassuring them that the bullying was not their fault, you are helping them to feel better about themselves. By encouraging children to deal with the bullying they are more likely to be able to move out of the victim role.

Help children to develop strategies to cope with bullying, including assertive behaviour

Children need to learn how to avoid the bullying and to learn to stand up for themselves. You can ask the child what he would like you to do to help him, including the offer of support whilst he approaches and confronts the aggressor.

Children can learn to think, look and act assertively and you can help them to find the words to respond to being threatened, called names, excluded or hurt. Small children can practise saying 'no' or 'I don't like it when you...' or 'Stop it now'. You can also encourage them to think about non-verbal communication including hand gestures, eye contact, posture and tone of voice. Older children will benefit from writing a diary to document the incidents, especially when bullying occurs on a regular basis.

Schools instruct children not to physically retaliate when they are attacked, although sometimes parents/carers will contradict this. No matter what you personally believe, as a member of staff you are required to accept school policy and to help children to stand up for themselves without resorting to violence.

Inform children of action being taken and by whom

Victims of bullying will be reassured by knowing that others are able to take control and deal with, or help them to deal with, the bullying. With more serious incidents you can inform the child whom you will be telling, and what is likely to happen.

Work with children who bully

Your policy is likely to describe zero tolerance towards bullying. Many schools recommend that incidents are dealt with swiftly and firmly, by using a range of strategies. These are likely to include the use of sanctions such as reprimand, detention, time out and missing treats. In the most serious cases parents may be involved and children may be excluded from school.

ACTIVITY 2

In your school:

What sanctions do you use when dealing with children who bully?

Is bullying discussed by your team, the children and other staff on a regular basis?

Bullying behaviour can make us feel very angry and it is tempting for adults to get their own back on the child who bullies. In fact children who bully often have serious problems including low self-esteem and poor self-control, and are likely to need as much help as their victim.

When working with children who bully, it is unhelpful to label individuals with terms like 'bully' or 'troublemaker' as this could lead to further problems. You will need to find a balance between setting extremely firm limits to ensure that the behaviour stops, whilst helping the child to take responsibility for their actions and to cope in more constructive ways. You should be clear, honest and direct with your response, avoiding humiliation, sarcasm or aggression. By dealing with bullying in this way, you are offering a positive role model. Children who bully often need to learn how to control themselves and to deal with their anger more constructively. Encourage them to develop empathy by putting themselves in the victim's shoes.

When faced with bullying behaviour, try to gain an account of what happened from the aggressor's point of view. If there is a group of children involved, it may help to talk to them individually. In the case of one-off, less serious incidents, you may impose a warning or a minor sanction. With persistent or more serious bullying you will be required to pass it to others to be dealt with. As already discussed, you are likely to benefit from discussion with the SENCO, class teacher or other experts to help you to understand the child's behaviour and the best way to deal with it.

Challenging discriminatory bullying

You will be required to challenge racist, sexist and anti-gay bullying as well as taunts made about children who are overweight or who have special needs. On occasions you may have to put your own personal opinions to one side and find ways to explain to children in age-appropriate language how distressing their comments and actions can be for the victim. Often small children repeat what they have heard without fully understanding the meaning of their words. Follow school guidelines for dealing with and reporting such behaviour.

Encourage bystanders to take action

Bystanders are people who stand by and let others get picked on. They are often afraid to become involved in case they are also targeted. The majority of people act as bystanders sometimes, and schools can encourage children to take a stand in many ways. For example:

> One school talked about this problem in assembly, and then encouraged children to role-play how they could show that they disapproved when they saw others bullying someone. LTSs continued this discussion informally in the playground.

Helping children to cope with friendship difficulties

Having a group of friends has been identified as an important protective factor against bullying. However, relationships sometimes go wrong and 20 per cent of children questioned stated that their tormentor was a former friend (Thomas Coram Research Unit 2003).

LTSs can help children to make friends and to deal with friendship difficulties. This means that you may have to tolerate the endless moans and complaints about who won't play with whom. Children need to be encouraged to sort out their differences without resorting to aggression or verbal abuse. Supervisors can help pupils without friends to form relationships by providing opportunities to be together and share common interests.

> In one school specific pupils were selected by LTSs to help with a project to improve the school grounds. Two initially friendless and bullied children, both known by a supervisor to be interested in wildlife, came together to help create a school garden.

ACTIVITY 3

Discuss with colleagues:

How do you help children to develop friendships, and to cope when things go wrong?

Regularly review playground organisation

There may be areas of your playground that are difficult to monitor and so you will need to keep moving or to position yourselves carefully. By improving the playground environment schools can reduce bullying. This will be explored in detail in Chapters 7 and 9.

Support existing playground initiatives

Playground buddy schemes involve older children befriending and supporting the younger pupils. Such schemes also have a positive effect on the whole school community and make it harder for children to stand by and let others suffer.

Consult the children on a regular basis

Involved schools consult with staff, children and their parents on a regular basis to gauge the extent and nature of the problem of bullying. This can happen verbally or by means of a questionnaire. Schools may also have a 'bully box', a box placed in an accessible place where concerns can be reported anonymously. An example of a bullying questionnaire is provided below.

You may decide to use this bullying questionnaire with the children. You will need to discuss this with your line manager and adapt the language depending on the age and understanding of the children.

Bullying questionnaire

	Boy	Girl
Are you a boy or a girl?	☐	☐

How old are you? ......

	Yes	No
Do you understand what bullying is?	☐	☐

	Yes	No
Have you ever been bullied at this school?	☐	☐

When you were bullied and what happened to you?...
....

Where were you bullied? ....

If you have been bullied, has it happened...	Yes	No
a) once?	☐	☐
b) occasionally?	☐	☐
c) often?	☐	☐
d) very often?	☐	☐

When you were bullied, who did you tell...	Yes	No
a) a friend?	☐	☐
b) a parent?	☐	☐
c) a teacher?	☐	☐
d) the lunchtime supervisor?	☐	☐
e) nobody?	☐	☐
f) anyone else?	☐	☐

	Yes	No
Have you ever seen anyone else being bullied?	☐	☐

When you see someone being bullied what can you do?...
....

What would help you to feel happier in the playground? ....
....

Thank you for answering these questions.

Bullying checklist for lunchtime supervisors

Consider the following questions and discuss your answers with your line manager.

Do you...	Yes	No
know your school anti-bullying policy and follow the procedure outlined?	☐	☐
make it clear to the children that bullying is unacceptable?	☐	☐
share information following incidents with all relevant staff?	☐	☐
receive information about children to keep a special eye on?	☐	☐
keep bullying on the agenda and encourage children to talk about it?	☐	☐
help victims to deal with bullying?	☐	☐
help children who bully to cope in a more constructive way?	☐	☐
create a climate where it's acceptable to tell an adult about incidents of bullying?	☐	☐
make yourself available to children and listen carefully to what children tell you?	☐	☐
at lunchtime check and supervise all accessible areas in the playground and toilets?	☐	☐
help children to cope with friendship difficulties?	☐	☐
review playground organisation to minimise bullying?	☐	☐
keep children constructively occupied in the playground?	☐	☐
receive appropriate training about recognising and dealing with bullying?	☐	☐

Conclusion

LTSs have an extremely important role in dealing with and preventing bullying. If you do this effectively you are likely to improve the lives of several of the children at school.

Finding out more

There are many organisations producing practical and useful information about bullying. They include:

Anti Bullying Alliance
www.nch.org/aba
Telephone 0207 843 6000

Anti Bullying Campaign
Telephone 0207 378 1446

Bullying Online
www.bullying.co.uk

ChildLine
www.childline.org.uk
Telephone 0207 239 1000

Don't Suffer in Silence
www.dfes.gov.uk/bullying

Kidscape
www.kidscape.org.uk
Telephone 0207 730 3300

CHAPTER 7

Play at lunchtime

Introduction

By doing your everyday job, you are likely to learn a great deal about children and their play. This chapter will explore how and why children play, and the important play opportunity offered by the lunchtime break. It will go on to examine playground organisation and a range of options that can be offered to pupils at lunchtime.

Until recently the lunchtime break was viewed mainly as a time for everyone to eat, for children and teachers to have a welcome rest from each other, and for children to let off steam to aid their afternoon concentration. Schools now recognise that, when well managed, the lunchtime session can also contribute to children's well-being, development and learning.

The importance of the lunchtime break

Due to changes in children's lifestyle, the school playground may now provide the only opportunity for some children to be physically active, and to play freely in an outdoor space. Children are often at home in front of televisions or computer screens. Many badly lack exercise and we are facing an obesity crisis. Parents are working longer hours and families are smaller, providing fewer brothers or sisters as playmates.

At lunchtime children benefit greatly from periods of relative freedom from adult control, when they can pursue friendships and create their own social worlds (Blatchford 1998).

What is play and why do children need it?

Play is active, often spontaneous, and can be done alone or with others. It is also a process which involves doing, exploring and testing out different types of behaviour. Play enables children to develop physically, socially, emotionally and intellectually. They can have fun, let off steam, interact, make friends and reduce boredom. It stretches thinking, creativity and imagination. Through play children develop necessary social skills including how to cooperate, negotiate, take turns and abide by rules.

Play can be therapeutic and helps children to cope with their powerful emotions. Children facing distress or trauma are likely to act it out in their play in an attempt to make sense of painful events.

The way children play

Children can play in many different ways depending on their physical needs, and their personality. Their play will also be influenced by their age, their stage of development and their gender. For example, very young children find it difficult to play with others without considerable adult input. As children get older they are more able to cope with complex rules and structured games.

Gender differences

ACTIVITY 1

Discuss the differences between the way girls and boys play.

In the playground boys tend to play in larger groups and are more physical. They are also more likely to argue about rules and leadership. Girls are more likely to play or talk in pairs or smaller groups, and are likely to be less aggressive (White and Wilkinson 2000). LTSs describe how girls' disputes can be complex and drawn out, often lasting for weeks and involving large numbers of children.

Types of play

Children need the opportunity for free unstructured play, in which they can be themselves, make their own decisions and play in their own way. On other occasions, particularly when they are over-excited or bored, they may need adults to structure the play by suggesting a game or an activity. Research suggests that, mainly for safety reasons, adults are at risk of over-controlling children's activities in the playground. Maintaining health and safety in the playground is a major priority and LTSs tread a fine line between keeping children as safe as possible, whilst allowing them to play in a free, exciting and challenging way. This will be explored further in Chapter 9.

According to White and Wilkinson, the most popular play includes rope games, ball games, physical contact games, imaginary play and some calmer 'walking about' activities. The majority of children's play involves physical contact, particularly in the case of younger children where rough and tumble and chasing make up a significant proportion of their games. The benefits and difficulties associated with such behaviour have been discussed in Chapter 6, page 57.

Creating a positive playground ethos

LTSs are key to creating a positive playground ethos. Playgrounds have been found to become happier places when:

- LTSs are offered training to enable them to interact and play with children.
- Children are offered appropriate play materials and types of playground activities.
- Playgrounds are zoned and offer a variety of activities.

Interacting and playing with children

There will be times when children are happily playing and need little adult intervention. On other occasions they may need your assistance. You are likely to make a considerable difference to the quality of lunchtime by introducing and teaching games.

When LTSs are actively and constructively involved in play, they are on hand to de-escalate conflict, channel play fighting into organised activities, act as positive role models for children who are struggling to sort out arguments, and to support isolated children. You can join in with children's play in a number of ways, ranging from turning a rope to teaching a new game. You can also make suggestions and initiate play when necessary, whilst allowing the children to make their own decisions whenever possible. How much you join in and stay in the game will depend on children's needs, and the demands on your time.

Teaching games

ACTIVITY 2

Can you remember the games you played in the playground when you were a child?

Would you be able to teach any of these to the children at school?

How could this be organised?

There has recently been an interest in re-teaching traditional playground games which you may wish to find out more about by contacting your local education authority and asking for the PE and school sports coordinator. Teaching children games can be demanding, and will need to be carefully paced. The game should be played often enough to familiarise the children, without becoming over-familiar and boring.

> An LTS described repeating a simple playground game for ten minutes, every day for a week, to familiarise the children. She then had a break, and returned to the game two weeks later. The children welcomed its return and remembered the rules well enough to join in quickly.

Can you play and supervise the playground at the same time?

Some LTSs will honestly say that they do not particularly want to play with the children although they are happy to offer support and help to pick up the pieces when things go wrong. Others describe the pressures of keeping children safe at the same time as attempting to play. One enthusiastic LTS described her experience in a busy infant school:

> I just get a game of skipping going, and am turning the rope when a child behind me has an accident, or a group of children start to fight. By the time I have sorted things out, the skipping activity that was going so well has collapsed and the children are arguing.

Schools may attempt to overcome this by employing a play leader with special responsibilities for play. Others recruit specific members of the LTS team to lead the play whilst others focus on supervising the playground. This requires an adequately staffed team, flexible practice and excellent organisation.

ACTIVITY 3

In your school how do you manage the conflicting demands of playing whilst supervising the playground?

How could things be improved?

Organised sport

Schools with adequate space and staff numbers may offer children the chance to participate in organised sports at lunchtime. A play leader or delegated LTS may have special responsibility for overseeing the activity, often organised on a rota basis in a particular area of the playground.

Competitive games and cooperative games

Competitive games such as football or netball have winners and losers. Children find it difficult to lose at any age, and for younger ones this can be particularly distressing. Although competition can act to motivate and challenge people, losing too often can have a negative effect. Children also benefit from playing cooperative games, which involve helping each other to achieve an agreed goal. Examples are skipping or circle games, where there are no winners or losers.

Inclusive play

When developing activities, you are required to plan to meet the needs of a wide range of pupils attending school. This may include boys and girls, able and disabled pupils, children with special needs, younger and less boisterous children.

ACTIVITY 4

Which groups of children do you think have the worst time in your playground?

How could this be improved?

How do you provide for the less boisterous and non-sporty children?

How do you ensure that the disabled or special needs pupils are included?

Does your playground interest the girls as much as the boys?

Below are some examples of practice developed by schools to include a wide range of pupils.

CASE STUDY 1

In one playground boys playing football dominated most of the space. The girls became marginalised and excluded. In response to this a meeting was called to discuss the problem with the children. It was agreed that football was to be restricted to a smaller area, and girls were offered female-only football once a week.

CASE STUDY 2

At a school which accommodated able bodied and physically disabled children, a separate soft-surfaced area was created in the playground so that children could play on the floor without being trampled by those participating in more boisterous activities. Both disabled and able-bodied children used this resource.

CASE STUDY 3

One school created a special, quiet playground zone for children who wanted to participate in 'calm activities'. A supervisor ensured that board games, drawing materials, books and construction toys were provided, and that children who wished to play more boisterously were directed to a different area.

Play with younger children

The playground can be a scary place for small children, who are likely to need support, nurturing and encouragement. Young children benefit from the security of developing close relationships with familiar supervisors.

Very small children may lack language or verbal communication skills, especially if English is not their first language or if they have special educational needs. You will need to check that the child has understood your communication, and be prepared to rephrase or act it out when necessary.

When supervising small children who are playing freely, it may help to observe the game, and to join in only when invited, or when you think it necessary. If possible, be led by the children and attempt to enter into their world, rather than trying to control the play. You can do this by watching carefully, and by asking the occasional question. Children are often happy to explain their play and to tell you what they would like you to do.

One LTS described how a small group of children invited her to hop over the leaves in the playground, which led to the princess's palace. She enjoyed joining in with the children's elaborate fantasy, and described how on one occasion she sought guidance from the players. At a later stage she made a suggestion to encourage the group to include a less confident child.

Nursery and reception children are likely to find organised or cooperative play difficult without adult input. When providing more structured play for them, you are aiming to help them to learn a range of activities and games. This may require breaking down the task to enable the children to develop the necessary skills.

When teaching a ball game, one LTS helped by regularly demonstrating the process in a circle. Once the children were able to catch the ball she had thrown to each one in turn, she then encouraged them to take turns to throw the ball to each other.

Often nursery and reception have separate age-appropriate playgrounds. When space is limited your school may decide to stagger the lunchtime to give the younger children time on their own.

Use of older children and buddies to support play

Children often benefit from mixing with other age-grouped pupils. Schools can recruit older buddies to interact and initiate play with the younger children. Such schemes are likely to need adult supervision.

Consulting children

For playgrounds to be successful, their organisation will need to be regularly reviewed and adapted. Mary Jackson (2004) from Learning Through Landscapes says:

> Your pupils are the experts. They should be involved in playground and playtime planning from the start. But you shouldn't ask them what they *want* in the playground, or you'd get a list of things like roller coasters. You should ask the children what they would like to *do* in the playground.

> In one school the LTSs consulted the younger children about preferred activities and dressing-up clothes were requested. These were collected from a range of sources and placed in a large box in the playground. Much to everyone's surprise, this became a great success even with some of the older classes.

Indoor play

Some children find a long time in the playground stressful, and schools are increasingly offering children the opportunity to attend lunchtime clubs and other indoor play provisions. Successful indoor facilities require organisation, space, staff and resources. They can offer a large range of activities including dance, drama, chess clubs, arts and crafts, computing and languages.

Conclusion

During lunchtime children benefit from the opportunity to play freely as well as having the chance to join in with more structured, organised activities. To supervise and initiate successful play at lunchtime you will need to develop a range of skills which you often don't use in other aspects of your work. For some LTSs this comes easily. For others you may need training and support. It is good to review your playground organisation and practice. Consider what is working well and what could be improved. A little imagination and creativity can go a long way.

Resources and relevant organisations

For up to-date information about play and playgrounds you can contact your local authority and ask for the PE and school sports coordinator.

Alternatively, you could try:

Active Playgrounds
A free guide for primary schools, British Heart Foundation
www.bhf.org.uk
Telephone 08450 708070

Everyone Can Play – inclusive play training pack
National Centre for Playwork Education
www.playwork.co.uk
Telephone 0870 120 6466

Games Kids Play
This is an American site that offers games from a range of countries.
www.gameskidsplay.net

Growing Schools
This is a major government programme to harness the full potential of the 'outdoor playground'.
www.teachernet.gov.uk

101 Fun Warm-Up and Cool-Down Games by John Byl
www.humankinetics.com

Learning Through Landscapes
LTL provide a range of relevant fact sheets and information packs to members.
www.ltl.org.uk
Telephone 01962 846258

Playground Games and More Playground Games by Rob Golding
www.pearsonpublishing.co.uk

Playground Pals
This is a fascinating website that provides international games, case studies and information about equipment and playground management.
www.pioneer.cwc.net/playgroundpals.htm

Primary Playground Development Pack
Youth Sport Trust
www.youthsporttrust.org
Telephone 01509 226600

Many of the above have been comprehensively reviewed by Howard Todd in his article 'Fun and fitness', 2 July 2004 in the *Times Educational Supplement*, www.tes.co.uk/search/story

CHAPTER 8

Managing wet play

Introduction

In the playground the weather takes on a whole new meaning. On windy days, just like animals, children run wild. An hour and a quarter can feel like an eternity on a cold November day, worse still when there are heavy scattered showers. Do you keep the children in, or let them out?

Wet play is unlikely to be an ideal situation, but can be manageable, and even enjoyable. In fact some children welcome the option of being inside, preferring it to the rough and tumble of the playground. This chapter will explore how schools and LTSs can work together to make wet play a positive experience. It will cover planning, preparation, practical organisation of space and staff, and the creative use of resources and activities.

Managing wet play

How do you cope with a hyperactive child within the confines of the classroom? How do you stay calm when trying to ensure that all children eat, are kept busy and safe, often in limited space, and possibly with an inadequate number of supervisors?

ACTIVITY 1

Here are some questions which will help you, and your team, to review the organisation of wet play. Allow yourself a few minutes on each question below.

- Do you have time to plan and prepare for wet play, and to review your practice?
- At what stage do you decide that it is too wet for children to be outside?
- Who decides that it is wet play and how is this communicated?
- How many classes are you required to supervise?
- During wet play, how successfully do you manage challenging behaviour?
- Where do you supervise the children?
- During wet play, what play equipment and resources do you have to keep the children occupied?

Planning and preparing for wet play

Finding time to plan wet play activities will make a real difference to the quality of the sessions. In practice there is not a great deal of time available to plan, and some teams use INSET days for this purpose, whilst others meet briefly before or after duty. Tasks to be tackled include reviewing existing arrangements, sorting equipment, photocopying activity sheets, or developing ideas for improvement.

Deciding it is wet play

Many schools will allow children to remain outside whilst it drizzles, although this is not always the case. Often the senior LTS or the school senior manager makes the decision to bring children inside and communicates this by using a whistle, bell, walkie-talkie or flag. Others rely on a manager or the senior LTS to tell everyone.

Supervising the dining room and the classrooms during wet play

You will need to carefully consider how many supervisors are needed to supervise the dining room, and how many this will leave to supervise the classrooms.

> In one school an LTS described how, during wet play, she often had to rush between three classrooms, on two different floors of the school building, to supervise the children. Classes were left without adult supervision for some minutes, posing health and safety risks.

See Chapter 9 for further health and safety discussions.

ACTIVITY 2

In your school how many LTSs supervise the dining room during wet play?

Does this leave enough supervisors free to manage the rest of the school?

Can the system be improved in any way?

Discuss your ideas and concerns with your line manager.

Managing children's behaviour

Tempers are more likely to flare when children feel cooped up and frustrated. Many of the practices described in Chapters 4 and 5 are relevant in these circumstances. It will also help for the wet play rules to be clear and on display. You will need to know how to get adequate management backup when necessary.

Where are the children supervised?

During wet play children are likely to be supervised in their own classroom. However, schools may be lucky enough to have libraries, spare classrooms or a separate dining room or hall to use. With adequate space you will have more scope to organise special activities which offer children exercise, stimulation and excitement. Without this space, you will have to work particularly hard to make the most of the existing facilities. Below are some examples of how schools have used the available space creatively.

> **CASE STUDY 1**
>
> Children took turns to use the hall to watch a video. Sometimes they participated in large group activities, including disco dancing, parachute games and team games. Those who did not wish to participate could stay in a supervised classroom.

> **CASE STUDY 2**
>
> Small groups of children volunteered to attend a board game club and a computer club held on rainy days in the school library and computer suite. An LTS and a learning mentor supervised the sessions.

> **CASE STUDY 3**
>
> Classes took turns to participate in a range of games and activities held under a weatherproof canopy in the playground, led by an LTS and a teaching assistant.

> **CASE STUDY 4**
>
> Volunteers from the whole of year 4 were able to attend a 30-minute craft activity, held in one of their classrooms, supervised by an LTS. Those who did not wish to attend were supervised in the other classroom. On another occasion they organised a singing session in a similar way.

> **CASE STUDY 5**
>
> An LTS organised a game of charades for the older children in the hall. On another occasion they played 'Just a minute' and had a balloon debate.

Clearly such activities require planning, team cooperation and careful supervision but the benefits are likely to outweigh the pressures.

Keeping children occupied

To achieve the best results you will need to:

- Build in time to plan and prepare for wet play activities
- Communicate clearly with the class teacher about the use of classroom equipment
- Create a collection of separate wet play equipment for each class
- Regularly update and swap this equipment between classes to provide novelty value
- Use your own entertainment skills
- Consider using older buddies to help with play for the younger children
- Try to ensure that the equipment and activities meet the needs of the wide range of children you supervise

Create a wet play box

Many schools create a wet play box for each class, which is stored safely and used only on rainy days.

A typical wet play box includes

- Paper/pencils/crayons
- Word sheets/colouring sheets, dot to dot
- Quizzes
- Board games
- A range of books
- Comics
- Card games

- Construction toys
- Videos/DVDs

You can make this more interesting by adding some of the following:

- Card (although this is expensive)
- Scrap boxes – collected from households and used to make models
- Plasticine and playdough
- Shoeboxes filled with objects for children to write or tell stories about (see case study below)
- Simple crossword or sudoku puzzles
- Connect Four
- Carefully selected catalogues, to be read or cut out
- Dressing-up clothes
- Miniature pool, snooker or football tables
- A source of music
- Wool/string
- Glue/scissors if considered to be safe
- Quizzes and sheets laminated with water soluble pens attached
- Traditional games, for example jacks or gobs

Regularly update and swap the equipment between classes.

Indoor games and activities

There will be occasions when children happily play with the equipment you provide. On other occasions you may need to initiate a specific activity or game to focus their attention or to calm them down. Some popular indoor games include:

- Simon says
- Wink murder
- Charades/acting/miming
- Noughts and crosses
- Head down thumbs up
- Hangman
- Singing games
- Memory games
- Sleeping tigers

Details of these and many more can be found in the play packages listed at the end of Chapter 7. More boisterous pupils will benefit from physical activities which can be offered subject to available space. Imaginative LTSs describe a wide range of additional activities that they use during wet play to interest the children, including:

> **CASE STUDY 1**
>
> An LTS put a range of unusual objects into shoeboxes, for example a feather, a pine cone and a small mirror. Teams of children were encouraged to make up or to write a story about the objects to be shared with the rest of the class. Her colleague organised a 'Show and tell' session followed by a video for the younger children.

> **CASE STUDY 2**
>
> An LTS entertained children for a whole lunchtime by offering a prize for the best portrait of her. On other occasions she organised competitions including timed puzzles using a stop watch, a talent competition, 'Draw the best cartoon character' and 'Design a poster'. The children helped her to judge the best efforts, and winners were awarded a small chocolate bar by the class teacher.

> **CASE STUDY 3**
>
> A group of year 6 children were allowed to dance to their own music in the classroom provided the noise level remained reasonable. When things became rowdy, a game of Wink murder was initiated.

> **CASE STUDY 4**
>
> Children were encouraged to make winter festival cards using card, glue sticks and magazine cuttings. Others were taught to fold paper to make simple animals and boats.

> **CASE STUDY 5**
>
> A group of reception children played a range of games such as 'Oranges and lemons' and 'The farmer's in the den' in one half of the classroom. Later they sang along with a nursery rhyme tape and played memory games.

Use your own entertainment skills

You are the most important resource available to the children. Think carefully about the particular skills you may have. Can you play chess or play an instrument? Can you sing or make paper models? You do not need to be an expert to have a go. Children are likely to respond to your ideas and enthusiasm.

Use the older buddies to help with play for the younger children

A number of schools use their buddies to assist during wet play. You will need to oversee their involvement and provide clear tasks. Never leave older buddies alone in a classroom to supervise younger pupils, though.

Ensure that the equipment and activities meet the needs of the wide range of children you supervise

This is never easy, as the majority of children usually would prefer to be playing outside. Ask them how they experience wet play and what could improve the experience. When choosing equipment and activities, as always, you will need to consider the age of the children, the needs of the boys and girls, as well as children with special needs. It is also advisable to select books, comics, dressing-up clothes and music which reflect a range of cultures.

ACTIVITY 3

Think of the children you find particularly difficult to keep occupied during wet play. Do they fit into a particular group? (For example, are they boys, girls, children of a particular age group, or children with special needs?)

Is there someone at school who could offer advice about these difficulties?

Conclusion

Wet play need not dampen your spirits. There is a lot you can do to make it a more positive experience for all involved. Hopefully, some of the ideas outlined in this chapter will help you to become more confident and adventurous in your wet play activities.

CHAPTER 9

Keeping children safe at lunchtime

Introduction

> There is no such thing as a completely safe play environment because there is no such thing as a safe child! Children will have accidents wherever they are. They will fall over each other, their feet and even over nothing at all.
>
> (Titman 1992)

During lunchtime, you are often dealing with large numbers of children who have been inside for several hours and have lots of energy. The concept of danger seems alien to many, and you are required to stop them doing things they desperately want to do. It is not surprising that, when attempting to keep children physically safe, you can sometimes feel like a 'Moaning Minnie'.

This chapter will explore measures you and your school can take to keep children safe at lunchtime in the playground and inside the school building. Your legal responsibilities will be outlined, as well as your role when assessing and managing risk, coping with accidents, administering first aid, recording incidents, and dealing with pupils' special needs.

Legal responsibilities

All school staff have a legal responsibility to keep themselves and others safe. The Health and Safety at Work Act 1974 places overall responsibility for health and safety on employers. In schools, this is shared by the local authority, the governors and the head teacher. If you wish to find out more, see Notes for managers, page 109.

As employees, LTSs have a responsibility to:

- Take reasonable care of their own health and safety whilst at work, and the health and safety of others who may be affected by their acts (including the children)
- Cooperate with their employers in health and safety matters
- Carry out activities in accordance with training and instruction
- Inform the employer of any serious risk

Assessing risk

What is risk assessment?

As part of your job you will be required to assess risks and take measures to reduce them. Whenever there are groups of people there will be an element of risk, as accidents can happen in almost any situation. Assessing risk involves deciding on the likelihood of an accident occurring within a particular set of circumstances. For example, you are likely to decide that letting children run in the playground is a 'low risk' activity, whilst letting children run in the dining room is a 'high risk' one. Consequently, you would expect to prevent children running in the dining room, but not in the playground.

To make good assessments about levels of risk, you will need to use common sense and life experience as well as some specialist knowledge, as demonstrated by the following example:

> During wet play, an LTS removed a jar of buttons from the reach of the nursery children as she decided there was a high risk that they would put the objects in their mouths, and possibly choke. With the junior school classes, she did not assess this as a high risk, so did not remove the jar unless she was supervising a class that included children with special needs.

In this example the LTS used her knowledge of child development, special educational needs and first aid to assess risk. In practice you are making these assessments every day.

Keeping children safe in the playground and the school building

The playground

In the playground large numbers of children move around relatively freely, and so accidents do happen. It is not surprising that LTSs may find keeping children safe stressful. One LTS described the pressure as follows:

I hate moaning and spoiling their fun, but looking after other people's children is such a serious responsibility. I feel sick at the thought of a child being seriously injured.

There is a fine balance between ensuring safety in the playground, whilst allowing children to play freely. As described in Chapter 7, it is normal for children to experiment, and to stretch their own physical limits. Children vary in their understanding of danger, and in their level of physical ability. When supervising them, it is tempting to err on the side of caution. This too can create problems. Wendy Titman believes that when children are over-restricted, they are likely to create more dangerous options 'out of frustration and boredom'. She concludes that, 'Helping children to understand the consequences of play behaviour and the nature of risk may improve their personal safety' (Titman 1992). This involves discussing with children the potential dangers involved in particular types of play, and exploring how the play could be made safer. Children can also benefit from guidance on avoiding accidents. Ultimately you are the adult and so will need to make the final decisions.

Thomson (2003) warns against a worrying trend in primary school playgrounds, mainly in response to health and safety concerns and fear of prosecution. She believes that staff are becoming over-protective and controlling, and that schools often have the philosophy 'When in doubt ban it'. This has sometimes resulted in the banning of activities like football, skipping, rounders, yo yos and playing with conkers. She fears that playgrounds are becoming 'barren, sterile and unimaginative places' and that spontaneous play; choice, creativity, and fun are being unnecessarily stifled.

ACTIVITY 1

Do you manage to find a balance between keeping children safe in the playground, whilst allowing them to play in an exciting and challenging way? If not what needs to change?

Other environmental factors which affect children's health and safety at lunchtime

Children require sufficient shade and water fountains to avoid the risk of sunburn or dehydration. The design and size of your playground may create potential dangers, especially if there are hidden corners, or dangerous structures such as spiked fences, and sheds with flat roofs to climb on. Accidents can be caused by broken play equipment, which will require regular inspection. Insecure playground boundaries and playgrounds with public access can also add to difficulties, especially if gates are left open or uninvited visitors enter the playground. For further discussion about playground security see Notes for managers, page 111.

ACTIVITY 2

Think about the playground you supervise. In the first column list examples of possible risks to children's safety in the playground at lunchtime. In the second column identify action that you or others take to reduce the risks.

Discuss your answers with your colleagues and line manager.

Risks to the children's safety in the playground	Action taken to reduce risk
Example:	
Faulty equipment. For example, a splintered wooden bat or a broken climbing frame.	I regularly check equipment and remove faulty goods. In the case of broken fixed equipment, I stop children using it and report this to the caretaker immediately to be fenced off and repaired. Continue until you have eight examples.

Your answers might include:

- Under-supervised areas of the playground, for example, a hidden corner which can be overlooked.

   Action: be vigilant and agree as a team how best to manage the problem. If difficulties remain, discuss these with your line manager.

- Children playing in a rough way.

   Action: learn to identify safe and unsafe play – see Chapters 6 and 7. Intervene when necessary. Remind children about the school rules for playing safely.

- Unsuitable equipment.

   Action: equipment needs to be maintained, for example, to avoid injury, children should be using soft balls instead of leather balls.

   Children need reminders about such expectations in assembly.

- Unclear playground rules; for example, children are not consistently challenged when they climb on fences, buildings and other 'forbidden' structures.

   Action: act consistently and remind children of playground rules. Expectations may need to be reinforced by senior managers.

- Inadequate security including a public right of way through your playground, gates that are left open, or gaps in the fence where objects can be passed to the children.

   Action: with the help of senior managers, reinforce the importance of playground safety to parents/carers. Politely challenge uninvited visitors in the playground, and direct them to the school office. Call for assistance if necessary.

- Unsafe car parking facilities. Children and vehicles sometimes share the same playground.

   Action: monitor carefully and feed back concerns to senior managers regularly.

If you are worried that issues passed on to be dealt with are not being acted upon, keep on voicing your concerns until you are satisfied with the outcome.

Keeping children safe inside the school building

LTSs supervise children in the dining room and in their classrooms during wet play. You may also supervise them in the medical room or during lunchtime clubs and detentions.

In the dining room

To enhance safety, schools can provide clear rules and routines for queuing, eating and the disposal of left-over food. There will need to be clear expectations about how children enter the dining room and where they sit. Children care as much about sitting with their friends as they do about what they eat, and you will need to strike a balance between keeping them safe whilst allowing them to socialise and eat together in a relaxed atmosphere.

During wet play

During wet play, you may have to leave children unsupervised in the classroom for short periods whilst attending to other classes. This is a cause for concern to be discussed with your line manager. Wet play equipment requires regular inspection and activities will need to be planned and monitored carefully. Try to consider the possible risks in advance and think of ways to reduce them. Activities may need to be stopped, amended or cancelled if they appear to be too dangerous or you have insufficient adults to supervise them.

ACTIVITY 3

Think about the times you supervise children inside the school building at lunchtime.

In the first column list several examples of possible risks to the children's safety inside during lunchtime. In the second column identify action that you or others can take to reduce risk. Discuss your answer with colleagues/line manager.

Risks to the children's safety inside the school at lunchtime	Action taken to reduce risk
Example:	
Children running into the dinning room.	I challenge and remind them clearly of the school rule about running. Teaching staff also reinforce this in assembly and in the classroom. Continue until you have eight examples.

Listed risks and action may include:

● Unacceptable behaviour in the dining room including running, shouting and pushing or poor table manners.

  Action: challenge assertively and refer children to the dining room rules.

- Unclear rules and routine for moving around the school building. For example, children run up and down stairs when coming inside from the playground.

  Action: challenge this and clarify your expectations. Request that expectations are reinforced by senior managers and teaching staff.

- Children entering the building having been given permission by teaching staff without your knowledge. This is obviously dangerous as they may be unsupervised, or unaccounted for in the case of an emergency.

  Action: discuss with your line manager to ensure that systems are in place to stop this happening.

- Faulty equipment or dangerous activities during wet play.

  Action: check equipment regularly and monitor the safety of activities.

- Insufficient numbers of LTSs to supervise classrooms during wet play.

  Action: discuss your concerns with your line manager, and review wet play arrangements regularly.

Training in health and safety matters

Your employer is required under health and safety law to provide training to ensure that you are competent to carry out your responsibilities. This may involve attending external courses or receiving school-based instruction. Children can also benefit from training in how to avoid accidents.

Coping with accidents and emergencies

Even in well-managed, safety-conscious schools, accidents and emergencies will happen. Having clear roles, procedures and well-prepared, competent staff can reduce the risk and the potential harm caused. To avoid panic and confusion, anticipate and discuss in advance how best to respond to various types of accidents and emergencies.

As illustrated by the following true incidents, school playgrounds are unpredictable places where exciting and amusing as well as tragic incidents take place.

- Much to the excitement of the children and staff, an emergency helicopter was forced to land in the junior school playground at home time, following a serious road accident nearby.

- A completely naked, mentally unwell man ran through a primary school playground, being hotly pursued by two uniformed police officers.

- A wild and dangerous looking dog managed to gain access to the playground at lunchtime, terrifying the children.

- A child became physically stuck in the playground climbing frame and had to be rescued by the fire brigade.

ACTIVITY 4

List several types of emergencies that you may be required to deal with.

1

2

3

4

5

6

Discuss with colleagues how you would respond to each of these situations.

When considering appropriate action, do you know:

How to raise the fire alarm?

Where the school fire exits are situated?

Set procedures for evacuating the school building?

How to access children's medical records when necessary?

How to administer basic first aid?

How to call for assistance when necessary?

Whose responsibility it is to call the ambulance?

How to challenge 'difficult' visitors to the playground?

If you are unclear about any of these points, seek clarification

Fire procedures

All LTSs will need to be clear about the school's fire procedures. Fire evacuation during wet play can be particularly difficult to manage as all the children are inside the building but without their class teachers. If your school does not practise their fire drill during lunchtime because of the disruption it causes you can suggest creating a mock scenario to practise these procedures. See Notes for managers, page 111.

Offering children reassurance

During and after emergencies, children who have been directly involved or who have witnessed distressing incidents are likely to need considerable comforting and reassurance. Some relevant skills have been outlined in Chapter 3. Children will differ greatly in the way they deal with their feelings and if you are unsure how best to respond, seek advice or refer the child on to someone appropriate.

First aid training

Your school is required to provide adequate and appropriate first aid equipment, facilities and qualified first aid personnel. They must also inform you of the first aid arrangements.

LTSs need to know who the appointed first aiders are, and when to pass on more serious matters to be dealt with. You will also require clear guidelines about dealing with children with special medical needs and disabilities, as well as issues relating to infection control and the use of medication including creams and plasters.

You may be invited by the school to train to become a qualified first aider. This entails completing and updating in-depth approved first aid training. Duties include:

- Giving immediate help to casualties with common injuries or illness and those arising from hazards at school

- When necessary, ensuring that an ambulance or other professional medical help is summoned

A government good practice guide entitled *Guidance on First Aid for Schools* (DfES 1998b) outlines roles and responsibilities in considerable detail.

ACTIVITY 5

Part A

Can you identify the qualified first aiders in your school?

Do you feel you have been offered adequate first aid training?

Do you have discussions about how to respond to children's minor or major accidents?

Part B

Discuss the following true case study. With hindsight, how should this accident have been dealt with?

A child collided with another in the playground at lunchtime, hitting her head and losing consciousness briefly. She then came round, sat up, lost consciousness again for a few seconds, came round again and stood up. The LTSs on duty made the decision to escort her to the welfare room. The welfare officer was new to the school and had very little first aid training. She was not informed at this stage that the child had lost consciousness twice in the playground. She phoned the child's mother and explained that her daughter had had an accident and needed to be collected. The mother came promptly and although her daughter was able to walk to the car, she lost consciousness some minutes later. The mother later sued the LEA for negligence.

Learning points from this incident:

- The child should not have been moved from the playground as she had suffered a potentially serious injury.
- An ambulance should have been called immediately, by either an LTS or the welfare officer. It could have been cancelled later, if no longer needed.
- The LTSs and the welfare officer should have had adequate first aid training.
- The welfare officer should have been called to the playground and given full details of what had happened.
- The mother should have been given full details about what had happened.

Recording and reporting accidents

By law, schools are required to record accidents in writing, usually in an accident book although in more serious cases a local authority or government accident form may also be completed. Following accidents you will also be required to inform other relevant members of staff as soon as possible, so that they can decide if there is further action to be taken. You can do this by word of mouth and by filling in an accident form. The information is often confidential and should only be discussed with the relevant people. If parents or carers approach you, unless you have been advised otherwise, refer them to the class teacher or senior manager.

Supporting pupils with specific medical needs

Some pupils will have medical conditions that require support so that they can attend school regularly. Your school is likely to have a policy on managing pupils' medication and on supporting their medical needs. Generally schools do not administer medication although exceptions may be made in special cases. You will need to obtain sufficient medical information about the pupils in your care, and you may require specialist training in a range of areas including responding to fits, using asthma pumps and epipens (necessary in some cases of severe allergic reactions). For more detailed information seek guidance from specialist staff. You can also read *Managing Medicine in Schools and Early Years Settings* (DfES 2005b).

When things go wrong

Sadly, things do occasionally go wrong and in extreme cases legal action may be taken against an LEA or school. Although it is rare, in theory action can be taken against individuals too. It is therefore crucial that you cooperate with your employers in health and safety matters, and carry out activities in accordance with training and instruction. If legal problems arise for employees, unions are an important source of advice.

Keeping yourself safe and healthy

Responsibility for looking after children and keeping them safe can be stressful. It is crucial that you also look after yourself at work and receive the necessary support and training to help you cope. This has been discussed in previous chapters and will be revisited in Chapter 10.

Conclusion

This chapter clarified your role and responsibilities when keeping children safe at lunchtime. Although thinking about accidents and emergencies can understandably make people feel anxious, it helps to remember that serious accidents and emergencies in schools are rare, and that LTSs usually do an excellent job when it comes to caring for and protecting children.

CHAPTER 10

Child protection

Introduction

Sadly, there might be children in your school who are being abused. They may choose to tell you, as a trusted person, about their unhappiness and mistreatment. Support staff often work closely with children, sometimes in intimate situations, and so may be in the 'front line' in detecting abuse. This chapter will explore how to recognise the signs, and how best to respond to protect children. It will examine your role and responsibilities, and explain how to protect yourself from false accusations of abuse at work.

Information about child abuse

What is child abuse?

Abuse is when a child or young person under the age of 18 is hurt or harmed by another person in a way that causes significant harm and which may well have an effect on their development or well-being.

ACTIVITY 1

When you hear about children being abused, how does it make you feel?

When learning about or dealing with child abuse, people often experience a range of powerful emotions including anger, disgust, sadness, depression and powerlessness. The idea and the reality of child abuse is often so dreadful that it is little wonder that school staff become emotionally involved, and sometimes deny that it is actually happening. You may find this subject distressing, particularly if you have personally experienced abuse. If so, it is advisable to seek support from someone you trust.

Who abuses children?

Child abuse takes place in every social class, race and religion. Statistics suggest approximately 90 per cent of all incidents are committed by someone the child knows, often within the family. Strangers do abuse children, but far less than is usually thought to be the case.

Sexual abuse is usually carried out by men, although women and teenagers also abuse children, usually within the home. Statistics suggest there is a greater risk of child abuse in families where parents or carers have a drug or alcohol problem, or where there is domestic violence.

Cultural differences

The way we raise and discipline our children will vary depending on our family and cultural rules. When working in a multicultural school you may notice such differences. For example, in certain societies it is normal to beat children as a form of discipline, whereas in England and Wales it is unlawful to hit children in a way that reddens their skin. In Scotland, using implements to chastise children, delivering blows to the head or shaking children is illegal. People will need to understand and abide by the child protection laws of their country of residence.

Child protection and the law

Children have a fundamental right to be protected from harm and abuse. All school staff have a duty of care and an important part to play in helping to protect children.

(DFES 2003)

The Children Act (1989) outlines the responsibilities of the local authority, schools and other organisations to ensure that children are protected from abuse. The DfES document *Safeguarding Children in Education* (DfES 2004) provides schools with current information and guidance.

Procedures in school

Your school's child protection policy

Schools are required to produce a child protection policy which outlines responsibilities and procedures for protecting children. This should include how to identify, respond to, report and record concerns. All staff should be given a written statement about the school's policies and procedures, and the name of the person to whom concerns should be reported (see below).

The designated senior teacher

Schools are required to appoint one or more 'designated senior teachers' (often, but not always, the head teacher) who have special responsibilities for dealing with child protection within the school. They are also responsible for advising staff and liaising with outside agencies.

Duty to refer

All school staff have a duty to report suspected abuse. You are *not* required to decide if the child is telling the truth, *nor* to investigate what has happened. Even if you feel uncertain or confused about a situation you are required to discuss your concerns or suspicions immediately. In some schools LTSs are expected to refer concerns to the senior LTS, where in others it may be the class teacher or senior designated teacher. If you don't know whom your school expects you to refer to, then find out now.

What if these concerns are not taken seriously?
If you are worried that appropriate action is not being taken, request feedback and state your concerns again. Your school has a responsibility to listen to you and to take your communication seriously.

What is likely to happen if a child is referred to social services?

If serious suspicions of abuse come to light, this will be reported to the social services department by the appropriate person within your school. Social workers are trained to interview children in specialised ways. If, following investigation, serious concerns remain, there are a number of options that can be taken. For further information you can obtain a free copy of *What to Do If You're Worried a Child Is Being Abused* (Department of Health 2003) from the DfES by phoning 0845 602 2260.

Sharing information about children who have been abused

Unless you are directly involved, you are unlikely to know which children are being investigated by the social services or monitored by the school. This confidential information will only be shared with a small number of staff on a 'need to know' basis.

LTSs often complain that they are kept in the dark, and that they would benefit from more information. One LTS spoke on behalf of her colleagues by saying:

> We don't need all the details, as we realise they are private. It would help to know which children are having serious problems. Then we could understand their behaviour better and make allowances.

ACTIVITY 2

Do you think you are given sufficient information about the children you work with?

If not, discuss what could help with your line manager.

Child protection training

All staff working in schools should be provided with child protection training relevant to their role. For LTSs, this could include guidance on how to:

- Recognise the signs of child abuse
- Listen to children
- Respond to concerns about a child's well-being as outlined by the school child protection policy
- Behave professionally at work to protect yourself from accusations of abuse

Each of these areas will be discussed below.

Recognising the signs of abuse

When working with children, you will need to know what signs and symptoms are indicators of abuse.

ACTIVITY 3

Can you name the four categories of child abuse?

They are physical abuse, sexual abuse, neglect and emotional abuse.

Physical abuse

A definition

> [A]ctual or likely physical injury to a child, or failure to prevent physical injury (or suffering) to a child including deliberate poisoning, suffocation and Munchausen's syndrome by proxy. [In Munchausen's syndrome by proxy, a person induces or falsely maintains for attention an illness or medical condition in another person, often a child.]
>
> (DfES 1995)

This is any form of physical injury inflicted, or knowingly not prevented. Physical abuse is sometimes known as 'non-accidental injury'.

Signs and symptoms

You may see marks on a child's body which are in unusual places and so are less likely to have been caused by accident, for example marks inside the child's thighs, behind the ears, around the groin. The shape of the marks can also give you clues; for example, they may resemble finger marks, burns, bites or those caused by straps or other objects. When you are tending to a child they may appear to be scared, as if waiting for the next attack, or have a tendency to unexpectedly flinch away from you for no obvious reason.

Children may directly tell you that they have been abused. This is known as a 'disclosure'.

> An LTS saw a large bruise on a child's neck partially concealed by his shirt. When she asked how it occurred, the child said, 'My uncle punched me'. The LTS listened carefully to the child's explanation and then immediately informed her line manager.

Sexual abuse

A definition

The actual or likely sexual exploitation of a child or adolescent. The child may be dependent and/or developmentally immature.

(DfES 1995)

Signs and symptoms

You may become concerned that a child's behaviour has become sexual in nature. They may touch you or other children inappropriately, act out adult sexual behaviour, draw inappropriate pictures, or say inappropriate things. You may get the feeling that 'something isn't quite right' and start to feel uncomfortable. Trust these feelings, and report your suspicions to the appropriate person without delay. Other signs to monitor are unexpected changes in a child's behaviour including them becoming withdrawn, aggressive, anxious or tearful. Sexually abused children may also develop a range of physical symptoms including urinary tract infections, frequent headaches and stomach pains, and bedwetting. They may self-harm, misuse substances such as glue or other solvents, or develop eating disorders.

Neglect

A definition

The persistent or severe neglect of a child, or the failure to protect a child from exposure to any kind of danger, including cold or starvation, or extreme failure to carry out important aspects of care resulting in the significant impairment of the child's health or development, including non-organic failure to thrive.

(DfES 1995)

Signs and symptoms

Children have the right to be fed, kept warm and cared for so that they can grow into healthy adolescents and adults. Neglect is the denial of these needs. Indicators can include children who are hungry, smelly, unkempt, dirty, constantly tired, inappropriately dressed, or who have untreated medical problems.

When working with children at school, we may have differing standards in relation to hygiene, appropriate clothing, healthy food and cleanliness. For example, you may be concerned that a child is wearing the same T-shirt for several days, or that his lunch box contains 'unhealthy' food. Although these concerns should be passed on, it does not necessarily mean a child is being neglected.

Here is one lunchtime supervisor's account of a child who *was* being neglected.

A year 2 child came to school regularly with a filthy lunch box containing a few slices of mouldy bread. The child was clearly hungry and I reported this to the head teacher immediately. I was told that the social services were involved with the family and I was asked to keep a written record of the content of child's lunch on a daily basis.

Emotional abuse

A definition

The actual or likely severe adverse effects on the emotional and behavioural development of a child, caused by persistent or severe emotional ill treatment or rejection.

(DfES 1995)

All abuse involves some emotional ill treatment. This category is used where it is the main or sole form of abuse. Children's behaviour and emotional development can be badly affected by verbal attacks, isolation, humiliation, over-protectiveness or extreme inconsistency in the behaviour of the parent or carer. Emotional abuse may also include persistent rejection, criticism, living in an atmosphere of fear and intimidation, being bullied or made a scapegoat.

(DfES 2003)

Signs and symptoms

Often children who have been emotionally abused will display severe behavioural difficulties. They are likely to have very low self-esteem and to be unable to form relationships with others. These children may bully, be socially isolated or display extreme attention seeking behaviour. They are also likely to develop physical problems similar to those described in relation to sexually abused children.

One LTS described a reception child who fitted this category.

I am often completely at loss about what to do to help her. She is rude, violent towards others, and all over the place. Although her behaviour often makes me feel very cross, I look at this tiny little person and it also makes me really sad – I can't imagine what she's been through.

Listening to children

As outlined in Chapter 3, LTSs will be required to listen to children in an open, non-judgemental and enabling way. You will also need to know how to respond sensitively to a child's concerns, who to approach for advice, and that you cannot guarantee complete confidentiality.

How children may tell you about abuse

Children might inform you about the abuse they are suffering in a number of ways. They may make a straightforward statement and describe what is happening, or make comments, or ask you questions. They may hint that something is wrong, or communicate this to you in a non-verbal way through their play or actions. Try to be sensitive to these communications and seek advice if you are unsure.

When a child tells you about abuse you should:

- Listen carefully without asking leading questions, giving your opinion, or putting words into the child's mouth.
- Accept what the child is telling you. You do not have to decide if it is true or not.
- Respond as calmly as possible to what the child tells you.
- Support and reassure the child, for example 'You have been brave to tell me. It's not your fault'.
- Assume they may have been threatened.
- Inform the child of what you will do and who you will need to tell.
- Inform the appropriate person and follow school procedures.

You should not:

- Make promises that you cannot keep, for example 'Everything will be OK'.
- Quiz the child about what happened. It is not your job to investigate.
- Promise that you will keep what you have been told secret (see below).
- Tell the child you do not believe them.
- Make any contact with the parent or carer – this is usually the social service's responsibility.
- Discuss the case with unauthorised people. If parents ask for confidential information, refer them to an appropriate member of staff.

Never keep secrets

ACTIVITY 4

What would you do in the following situation?

A year 6 girl told an LTS that she would like to tell her about something 'bad happening to her', but could only do so if the LTS promised not to tell anyone else. The LTS explained why she could not make this promise and encouraged the child to tell her what was happening anyway. The child refused to say any more.

Children may ask you to keep secrets. They may have been threatened by their abuser or told that what is happening must not be talked about. You will need to explain that if they are being harmed, you must pass it on, so that they can be helped. Children usually accept this.

In the above case study, the LTS needed to encourage the child to talk by trying a range of strategies. She could explain that she is unable to help the girl if she doesn't know what is happening, and could praise the child's bravery for talking to her in the first place. She could ask the child if there was anyone else she would be able to talk to, and show the child she understands how hard it can be to trust others.

The LTS would also need to report this discussion to an appropriate person even if she was not given any more information (see Duty to refer on page 91).

Recording incidents of abuse

Your school will have clear procedures for recording incidents of abuse. You will be required to write down the facts of what you saw or were told as soon as possible, using the child's own words when appropriate. If you find writing difficult, you can request assistance. The record should be signed, dated and kept in a confidential place.

Helping children to become aware of their personal safety

There is a great deal you and your school can do to help children to become more assertive, and to resist unhelpful pressures. Ideas have already been discussed in previous chapters. If you wish to learn more, talk to your line manager or SENCO.

Professional conduct and appropriate physical contact

To ensure high professional standards, and to avoid unfounded accusations being made, you will need to think carefully about how you conduct yourself at work.

ACTIVITY 5

Identify situations at work when you may be particularly vulnerable to being falsely accused of abuse. What precautions do you take to minimise the risk?

LTSs need to take particular care to follow relevant school policies and guidelines in relation to:

● Offering children intimate care

● Appropriate physical contact with pupils

Offering children intimate care

As part of your job, you may be required to intimately care for pupils including those who have had toileting accidents or have been physically injured. If you work in special schools you may also be required to intimately care for pupils with physical disabilities. To avoid leaving yourself vulnerable, you will need to know and to follow relevant school policies, codes of conduct and guidelines.

Appropriate physical contact with pupils

Your school is likely to have a policy on appropriate physical contact. The use of reasonable force to physically restrain pupils has been discussed in Chapter 5. Many LTSs feel strongly that they cannot do their job properly without using some physical contact. Government guidelines accept that you may also need to touch children if they are in distress and need physical comforting. They suggest that staff should use their discretion and be aware that some children may be particularly sensitive to physical contact because of their cultural background or because they have been abused. Guidelines also recommend clear practices are agreed upon where staff and pupils are of different sexes, and suggest that it is inadvisable to touch adolescent pupils. Also 'staff need to bear in mind that even innocent actions can sometimes be misconstrued' (DfES 1998a).

Many head teachers and LEAs recommend that this type of physical contact should be initiated by the child, and that you should never kiss or cuddle children, nor allow them to sit on your lap. Other good practice may include encouraging children to dress and undress themselves, keeping the door open, and having two members of staff present when you examine or care for children. Support staff often have strong opinions about this subject and you may welcome the chance to seek clarification and up-to-date information from your line manager.

Conclusion

It is essential that all school staff keep an open mind, listen carefully to children, follow school policies and procedures, and work together to protect the children in their care.

Part 2

Notes for managers

Introduction

This part of the book is written for managers within the school, particularly for those who line manage LTSs or oversee the lunchtime break. Each section below should be read in conjunction with the relevant chapter in Part 1.

There is a large amount of information in this book – more than most managers or LTSs will be able to retain in their day-to-day work. Consequently, you may wish to consider drawing up a set of 'simple rules' with LTSs. This involves describing in very succinct and memorable sentences how they are to undertake their duties. The beauty of simple rules is that they provide a clear framework for doing the job. The best ones are short, and small in number. For example:

Always be child-centred

Plan for good behaviour

Keep everyone safe

Seek help when necessary

Chapter 1 The role and responsibilities of the lunchtime supervisor

Chapter 1 offers an overview of LTSs' roles and responsibilities. The issues of accountability and confidentiality within the school community are also discussed. The chapter ends by focusing on the importance of lunchtime staff being valued by the school community. The five activities can be used to ensure LTSs are clear about their role and the expectations of others.

Who supervises at lunchtime?

For lunchtime to run smoothly, schools will need an adequately staffed and well-managed team of LTSs. There are no nationally agreed guidelines stating the number of LTSs to be employed by each school, and some head teachers decide to fund an LTS for every class in the school, believing that the advantages outweigh the financial pressures. Others employ teaching assistants, or a mixture of teaching assistants and

LTSs to supervise lunchtimes, believing that this improves efficiency and the quality of relationships. As explored further in Chapters 1 and 2, effective management of the LTS team can improve efficiency.

Clarifying roles and responsibilities

To help clarify their roles and responsibilities, all LTSs will need access to:

- User-friendly summaries of school policies in relation to behaviour, health and safety, child protection, bullying, inclusion, confidentiality, physical contact. Meeting time may be required to help team members understand how these policies apply to them in practice. One head teacher described how he drew up specific, bullet-pointed summaries of relevant policies to help with this process.
- An up-to-date job description.
- An induction pack or notes outlining expectations. In some schools this is prepared by the senior LTSs and in others by the line manager.
- Regular discussions with a line manager, to reinforce good practice and to clarify issues of responsibility, accountability and confidentiality – see Chapters 1 and 2.

Accountability and confidentiality

LTSs will benefit from clear channels of accountability. This is discussed on page 8 of Chapter 1. Activity 3 is aimed to help develop thinking in this area.

Confidentiality is discussed in detail in Chapter 1, page 10. Activity 5 on page 11 helps you and your LTS team explore this important subject further. Managers may need to help LTSs to decide how best to respond to parents' everyday enquiries about their children's eating and behaviour, and when to refer the parent to teaching staff for further discussion. See page 11, Chapter 1 for a brief discussion.

Managers regularly have to decide how much information to share with LTSs about the children they work with. It can be difficult to find the right balance between providing sufficient information to enable LTSs to work well, whilst respecting the child's right to confidentiality. This is discussed in greater detail in Chapter 2 and in subsequent chapters.

The role of the senior LTS

A strong senior LTS can enhance team effectiveness, improve communication and staff morale, and consequently make the manager's job easier. Difficulties arise, however, when an unsuitable person has been appointed, often on the basis of long service as an LTS, rather than the potential to fulfil a supervisory role. Many schools under-use the senior LTS, and fail to fully recognise their management potential. Senior LTSs often benefit from further training in basic management skills.

Valuing lunchtime supervisors

As with the pupils, the way LTSs are treated within the school will have an effect on their self-esteem and confidence. On a whole school, systemic level, the way that support staff are treated is an important indication of how your institution values its least powerful members. To be an effective role model, hopefully managers *will* develop relationships with LTSs in a way that demonstrates how you would like *them* to relate to the children.

Chapter 1 describes how LTSs can gain the respect of other staff and children by behaving in an accountable and professional manner.

Schools can reinforce their status and authority by:

- Ensuring that the school community are clear about the LTS's role and responsibilities. See Chapter 1, Activities 3 and 4, pages 7 and 9.
- Creating systems of reminding children and parents of the authority and importance of the LTS role.
- Having expectations that all staff will treat LTSs with respect regardless of whether children are present.
- Considering how LTSs are to be referred to – are they known as the dinner ladies, even if this isn't their job? Are they called by their first names when other staff are referred to by Mr or Mrs, followed by their surnames?
- Putting pictures of all staff including the LTSs on display in the school reception.
- Including LTSs at school events (for example, by inviting them to school concerts, outings or staff social events). See examples of bad practice, Chapter 2, page 13.
- Linking particular LTSs with individual classes or year groups to improve their relationships and status.
- Providing LTSs with appropriate guidance communication and training. This has been addressed throughout this book.
- Offering LTSs the opportunity to develop skills to work in other roles and capacities within the school in line with workforce remodelling.

Chapter 2 Communication systems within the school

Chapter 2 considers how in the light of many LTSs' short working hours, schools have to create and implement tailor-made systems to ensure a two-way structured exchange of information.

Information about the school – a checklist

Are there systems in place to ensure the following...	Yes	No
all LTSs receive the school newsletter and other relevant letters, list and minutes?	☐	☐
information is regularly distributed and updated?	☐	☐
LTSs are informed about staff changes and are introduced to new staff members?	☐	☐
LTSs are informed about changes in school rules and routines?	☐	☐
communication is timed appropriately to avoid LTSs learning about changes from the children?	☐	☐
LTSs are informed about school events including fundraising initiatives, special assemblies, staff outings or lunches?	☐	☐
that LTSs have forums to feed back their ideas and concerns?	☐	☐

Information about the children

The amount of information and detail shared about the children with LTSs is likely to be decided on 'a need to know' basis and appropriate confidentiality will be at the forefront of a manager's thinking. LTSs often feel they are given insufficient amounts of information about the children to do their job effectively.

Are LTSs provided with the following...	Yes	No
a list of children's special medical needs, displayed in a confidential place?	☐	☐
an up-to-date list of children's special dietary requirements, placed in an appropriately accessible place?	☐	☐
sufficient details about children's special educational needs? This may be discussed in meetings with other staff members or communicated in writing.	☐	☐
information about children who are bullying or being bullied?	☐	☐
strategies for managing children with particularly challenging behaviour? Again this may involve discussion with other staff members including the SENCO.	☐	☐
information about circumstances that may be affecting children including family problems?	☐	☐
systems to ensure that LTSs can pass to the appropriate people information about children's behaviour and well-being?	☐	☐

Meetings

Meetings are a crucial means of communication. They can, however, be time consuming and costly. Chapter 2 explores what types of meetings can be beneficial and how frequent they should be. Best practice suggests that LTSs should be paid for attending all essential meetings.

Meetings checklist

Do you offer LTSs meetings...	Yes	No
with the head teacher or another delegated line manager on a regular basis?	☐	☐
with the class teacher if relevant?	☐	☐
with the SENCO to discuss specific pupils' special educational needs and behaviour?	☐	☐
with their key stage team?	☐	☐
with their peer group (comprising the LTSs and the senior LTS without senior managers being present)?	☐	☐
with the whole staff group when relevant?	☐	☐
with the senior LTS on a regular basis and expect them to liaise with the rest of the team?	☐	☐

	Yes	No
to allow sufficient time for issues to be discussed?	☐	☐
to value your LTSs by paying them overtime to attend meetings?	☐	☐
to encourage LTSs to share the responsibility for organising and contributing to meetings?	☐	☐
to encourage LTSs to voice their opinion as well as using the time to share information?	☐	☐
to invite LTSs to attend relevant whole staff INSET days?	☐	☐

Written communication

Providing adequate written communication is an effective way to ensure that information is shared. Bear in mind that the literacy skills within the team are likely to vary.

Do all LTSs have access to the following…	Yes	No
regularly distributed and updated communication that is written in simple, jargon-free language?	☐	☐
the school newsletter?	☐	☐
lists of dates of school term, INSET days and other important staff events?	☐	☐
minutes from relevant meetings (or parts of meetings)?	☐	☐
a message or briefing book providing information by teaching staff about children's needs or difficulties?	☐	☐
lists of children's medical needs, allergies and dietary needs?	☐	☐
a daily staff briefing if appropriate?	☐	☐
an up-to-date list of children attending lunchtime clubs, outings and any other relevant activities?	☐	☐
the detention book?	☐	☐
forms, slips or books to be used to pass information between LTSs and other staff including the office staff and the site manager/caretaker?	☐	☐
copies of relevant guidelines, policies and procedures, possibly in summary form?	☐	☐
written communication placed in an accessible location?	☐	☐
their own notice board, pigeon hole or message book?	☐	☐

The handover of information before and after lunchtime

A two-way structured exchange of information before and after lunchtime will help to ensure that relevant facts are shared and acted upon. Children will consequently view the lunchtime as a consistent part of the school day. See Chapter 2, page 19 for a full discussion.

Feedback following serious incidents

Following serious lunchtime incidents, LTSs need to know what happened and how the children were dealt with. Such feedback can alleviate the regularly voiced concern that not enough is being done. Managers can also encourage LTSs to ask for information rather than to wait passively for it.

A staff debriefing

LTSs often benefit from the opportunity to meet together informally for a few minutes at the end of lunchtime to share experiences and discuss incidents. This offers peer support and can help to reduce stress. LTSs are sometimes but not always paid for this time.

Chapter 3 Building positive relationships with children

This chapter outlines a range of skills and practices to help LTSs to develop positive relationships with the children they supervise. The eight activities can be used to encourage the acquisition of skills in areas that include being child-centred, encouraging, a good listener and an effective communicator. The chapter concludes by exploring factors that interfere with positive relationships and how to overcome these hurdles.

Developing LTSs' understanding of the factors that affect children's lives

Helping support staff to understand the issues affecting children's lives can help them to relate to children with greater sensitivity. This can be achieved by inviting them to special school celebrations, assemblies or training sessions.

Organisational issues

The Primary National Strategy document *Playtimes and Lunchtimes* (DfES 2005a) describes developing 'systems to link particular lunchtime staff with particular classes or year groups, so they are part of the class or year group team'. This has obvious advantages when it comes to developing relationships with children and can create a sense of belonging for LTSs. Managers will need to help LTSs to avoid over-identifying with their class or group at the expense of the other children.

The chance to observe good practice

LTSs who are not also teaching assistants do not have many opportunities to observe skilled teaching staff interact with children in the playground or in the classroom. Some schools believe the benefits of such observation are so great that they pay their LTSs to work in the classroom for a limited period. It will help if teachers or managers can engage in regular discussions to explain how they are attempting to sustain relationships with the most challenging children. Pairing an inexperienced LTS with a more experienced member of the LTS team can also be helpful.

Chapters 4 and 5 Managing behaviour at lunchtime

Notes for Chapters 4 and 5 have been amalgamated.

Chapter 4 examines strategies and whole school practices that can be developed to encourage positive behaviour at lunchtime. It also explores some of the underlying reasons for children's misbehaviour and outlines a number of theories that have influenced behaviour management in schools. The nine activities, the checklists and the behaviour management case studies on page 34 can be used in training sessions.

Chapter 5 explores a whole school model of behaviour management and effective strategies to deal with and challenge unacceptable behaviour. The chapter concludes by focusing on coping with verbal abuse and violence. There are three activities which include a number of discussions and case studies to be used to develop staff knowledge and skills.

Lunchtime is likely to be most successful when LTSs are consistently working alongside other staff members to manage children's behaviour. Schools on the other hand must agree on clear and consistent rules and routines so that all staff members 'sing from the same song sheet'. This requires regular whole school discussion, feedback and review of practice. Chapters 4 and 5 explore how to achieve a high standard of behaviour management at lunchtime, and schools will need to:

- Have an adequately staffed and well managed team of LTSs.

- Use INSET days, training sessions and meetings to focus on consistently implemented behaviour management strategies and policies.

- Make the behaviour policy accessible and understandable to LTSs.

- Encourage LTSs to be assertive, proactive and to plan for children's good behaviour at lunchtime (see Chapter 4, page 41).

- Ensure that LTSs use a range of strategies to encourage positive behaviour (see Chapter 4, page 38).

- Encourage LTSs to develop positive relationships with children and to manage behaviour in a way that minimises confrontation (see Chapter 3 and Chapter 5, page 48).

- Agree what constitutes unacceptable behaviour and ensure that the consequences are clear and sanctions are consistently implemented.

- Share relevant information about the children on an ongoing basis.

- Offer support, training and senior management backup to help LTSs to cope with the most challenging behaviour.

- Manage some of the physical and environmental issues that affect children's behaviour (see Chapter 4, page 43).

- Help LTSs to encourage children to take responsibility for their own behaviour (see Chapter 4, page 43).

- Provide excellent role models for their staff (see Chapter 4, page 43).

Behaviour management checklist

In school...	Yes	No
is there an agreed range of rewards, consequences and sanctions for unacceptable lunchtime behaviour?	☐	☐
are LTSs helped to use rewards and sanctions in a reasonable and consistent way (see Chapter 5, page 46)?	☐	☐
Do LTSs have autonomy to distribute rewards during the lunchtime break?	☐	☐
Are systems in place to ensure that there is consistent practice during playtimes, lunchtimes and during other times of the day?	☐	☐
Is LTSs' authority undermined by contradiction or inappropriate intervention by other staff members?	☐	☐
Are 'time out' sanctions in place and used consistently?	☐	☐
Is there an indoor 'cool down' space (such as a detention room)?	☐	☐
Are there systems to provide LTSs with feedback on the outcomes of more serious incidents?	☐	☐
Are systems regularly discussed and reviewed?	☐	☐

Offer special support, training and senior management backup to help LTSs to cope with the most challenging behaviour

You can...

- Inform LTSs of suitable strategies to be used with particular children. See discussion, Chapter 5, page 46.

- Implement special lunchtime arrangements, including indoor provisions and extra support for troubled children or structured backup systems for the LTSs. This has been explored in greater detail in Chapter 5.

- Create systems to ensure there is backup from senior managers in the playground or in the dining room when necessary. See discussion, Chapter 5, page 51.

- Encourage LTSs to conduct themselves in a professional manner. See Chapter 5, page 52. This will include discussions about what constitutes acceptable physical contact with pupils.

- Offer LTSs support when they have been hurt or seriously verbally abused by pupils. See discussion in Chapter 5, page 52.

- Encourage LTSs to explore ways to conduct themselves professionally, even when facing extremely provocative behaviour from pupils. See discussion, Chapter 5, page 53.

Chapter 6 Dealing with bullying

Chapter 6 explores the complexity of the problem of bullying including what constitutes bullying, who is likely to bully or be bullied, and the devastating consequences for the victims. The chapter also looks at what schools can do to deal with this problem at lunchtime, both on a whole school and on an individual level.

Offering LTSs appropriate anti-bullying training

Bullying: Don't Suffer in Silence (Smith 2000), a DfES anti-bullying pack for schools, provides a useful range of information for all staff and can be used to train and inform staff.

For a full list of relevant training topics for LTSs in this subject see Chapter 6, page 63. LTSs will also need to be aware of the school policy and procedures for dealing with bullying – see Chapter 6, page 57. Finding relevant anti-bullying training can be difficult and your LEA may be able to provide input. To initiate further discussion, managers may wish to encourage LTSs to complete the bullying checklist included at the end of Chapter 6 and to respond to their comments.

Recommend a range of strategies to identify and deal with bullying which can be adapted to fit the circumstances. This has been discussed in Chapter 6, page 57. LTSs will also need to know in which circumstances they are expected to deal with incidents of bullying themselves, and when, in more serious or persistent incidents, to pass details on to others to be dealt with. When dealing with children who bully, managers may need to help LTSs to understand that the child is likely to have problems. See discussion in Chapter 6, page 60.

Developing the playground

As discussed in Chapters 6 and 7, developing the playground can decrease the incidents of bullying.

A playground checklist for managers

Does the school…	Yes	No
have a positive anti-bullying ethos?	☐	☐
review playground supervision on a regular basis?	☐	☐
ensure all areas of the playground are supervised, especially areas that are hard to see?	☐	☐
have clear procedures for supervising the toilets when necessary?	☐	☐
train supervisors to recognise and respond to bullying?	☐	☐
ensure that boredom is kept to a minimum by providing equipment or structured activities?	☐	☐
zone the playground to decrease marginalisation or isolation of children?	☐	☐
introduce playground initiatives to create an anti-bullying ethos?	☐	☐

Chapter 7 Play at lunchtime

Chapter 7 outlines the importance of the lunchtime break in offering children constructive play opportunities. It also explores how to develop a positive playground ethos by having a well-trained team of LTSs with the skills to facilitate play when necessary and the wisdom to know when to leave children to their own devices. The chapter addresses the provision of appropriate playground equipment and activities, and the organisation of the playground. The four activities and the case studies included can be used to review existing practice and to develop inclusive play at lunchtime.

The role of the LTS

Lunchtime staff will vary greatly in their desire and ability to initiate, facilitate and to physically play. The number of LTSs in post is also likely to impact on their capacity to involve themselves, at the same time as keeping the children safe. Managers may consider recruiting a play leader or delegating play responsibilities to teaching assistants or more enthusiastic team members (see Chapter 7, page 67).

The way children are encouraged to play is an important consideration. Researchers such as Thomson and Blatchford outline a worrying trend for schools to adopt a 'constraining and interventionist' stance (see Chapter 7, page 66).

Training for LTSs

Facilitating children's play requires special skills, which differ considerably from those needed by LTSs in other areas of their work. Specialised training is discussed in Chapter 7, page 66.

Providing playground equipment and activities

This is discussed in detail in Chapter 7, page 68. The checklist below summarises many of the issues.

Does your school...	Yes	No
build in time to plan for playground games and activities?	☐	☐
offer a variety of playground equipment and activities?	☐	☐
have equipment that is suitable for a range of children, including those with disability?	☐	☐
provide adequate and accessible storage space for playground equipment?	☐	☐
have systems for maintaining, checking, distributing and collecting, and replacing playground equipment?	☐	☐
offer a range of activities to meet the needs of different pupils?	☐	☐
ensure that football does not dominate the playground?	☐	☐
offer initiatives to encourage children to take responsibility for caring for playground equipment?	☐	☐
consult and actively involve pupils in relation to the available activities and equipment?	☐	☐
rotate the playground equipment and activities to provide novelty value?	☐	☐
recruit a play leader or appropriate staff members to initiate games and activities?	☐	☐
encourage buddies to play with the younger children?	☐	☐
review playground activities on a regular basis?	☐	☐
budget and fundraise to finance the equipment?	☐	☐
involve LTSs and parents in fundraising initiatives?	☐	☐

A playground organisation checklist

	Yes	No
Is the playground a welcoming place which inspires a sense of wonder, excitement and respect (Titman, 2002)?	☐	☐
Is the playground zoned to include an area for active play, quiet activities, sports, imaginative play, etc.?	☐	☐
Is the playground marked to encourage imaginative play?	☐	☐
Are there netball or basketball hoops and other fixed equipment?	☐	☐
Are there seats, benches, dens and other interesting structures?	☐	☐
Does the playground have an out of bounds area and if so is it really necessary?	☐	☐
Is there fixed equipment such as climbing frames?	☐	☐
Is there a covered play area?	☐	☐
Does the playground have art to provide colour and texture?	☐	☐
Are there an adequate amount of trees or flowers?	☐	☐
Are there adequate water fountains, litter bins and shade?	☐	☐
Does playground zoning unnecessarily limit the children's freedom?	☐	☐
Would you spend time in your school grounds if you didn't have to?	☐	☐

Resources

A list of resources about playgrounds and playground games is included at the end of Chapter 7.

Chapter 8 Managing wet play

Chapter 8 covers planning, preparation, practical organisation of space and staff, and the creative use of resources and activities for wet play. Ideas for games, activities and the content of wet play boxes are also included.

Organising wet play

Consider the numbers of LTSs available to oversee wet play, and how they can adequately cover supervision of the dining room and the classrooms (and/or other rooms occupied by the children). You should assist LTSs to manage the existing space flexibly, and to accurately assess and manage the risk of wet play activities (see Chapter 9). Behaviour management can be particularly challenging during wet play and LTSs need to know how to access your support and backup when necessary. Also see Chapters 4 and 5.

A manager's wet play checklist

During wet play do you...	Yes	No
have clear systems to decide and communicate that it is wet play?	☐	☐
have systems of communication between the teachers and the LTSs clarifying what classroom equipment can be used?	☐	☐
have adequate numbers of LTSs to supervise the classrooms and the dining room?	☐	☐
manage the available indoor space constructively?	☐	☐
provide specific wet play equipment and imaginative activities to occupy the children?	☐	☐
ensure that this equipment is suitable for the range of different pupils attending your school?	☐	☐
regularly update and swap the equipment between classes to provide novelty value?	☐	☐
consider a range of ways to fund wet play equipment?	☐	☐
have clear wet play rules and routines on display to be referred to?	☐	☐
provide LTSs with guidance on how best to supervise children with behavioural difficulties or special educational needs?	☐	☐
use older buddies to help with the younger classes?	☐	☐
offer management backup when necessary?	☐	☐
provide clear guidelines to ensure that children remain safe during wet play?	☐	☐
build in planning and review time for your wet play activities?	☐	☐
ask the children how they experience wet play and what could improve the experience?	☐	☐
encourage LTSs to use their skills and talents to entertain the children constructively?	☐	☐
provide wet play clubs?	☐	☐

Chapter 9 Keeping children safe at lunchtime

Chapter 9 explores measures schools can take to keep children safe at lunchtime in the playground and inside the school building. Legal responsibilities are outlined, as well as the role of the LTS in assessing and managing risk, coping with accidents, administering first aid, recording incidents, and dealing with pupils' special needs.

The school's responsibilities

For schools, the legal responsibilities for employers and employees under the 1974 Health and Safety at Work Act are outlined in the DfES 2001 Guidance 0803/2001 *Health and Safety: Responsibilities and Powers*. A comprehensive list of up-to-date and relevant health and safety guidelines and information can be obtained from the Teachernet website at www.teachernet.gov.uk.

The health and safety policy

Under the same Act, employers must have a health and safety policy, and employees must be consulted and made aware of their roles and responsibilities as defined in it. As always LTSs are likely to require your support in accessing relevant parts of the policy.

Training for LTSs in health and safety matters

The employer is required by law to provide health and safety training to ensure that staff are competent to carry out their responsibilities.

Relevant training for LTSs could include:

- Risk assessment
- Initiating safe play
- Coping with accidents and emergencies at lunchtime
- Playground security
- First aid
- Fire procedures
- Recording and reporting incidents
- Working with children who have special medical needs

All the above topics have been discussed in detail in Chapter 9. Some will be briefly discussed below.

Initiating safe play

This has been discussed in Chapter 9, page 81. LTSs may require assistance to find a balance between allowing children to play in a stimulating way, whilst keeping them safe. Although tempting, the risks of always erring on the side of caution and over-restricting children have their own set of problems.

Chris Lowe, *TES* Legal Editor, says:

> The risk to children during break time has always been there, and short of clear and gross negligence...the courts have striven to uphold the rights of children to learn from play. Health and safety laws do not require schools to ban everything remotely dangerous. Schools need to consider risk that is 'reasonably foreseeable' and to take 'reasonably practicable' steps to avoid or to minimise them.
>
> (Northern 2004)

Coping with accidents and emergencies at lunchtime

Accidents and emergencies will happen. Having clear roles, procedures and well-prepared, competent staff can reduce their risk and the potential damage caused. Activity 4 on page 85 encourages LTSs to anticipate and discuss in advance how best to respond to a range of accidents and emergencies.

Playground security

Details of the Working Group on School Security (WGSS) recommendations can be found on the Teachernet website. A DfES commissioned research report *School Security Concerns* (Lloyd and Ching 2003) also makes interesting reading.

First aid training

All LTSs will require basic first aid training to ensure they are able to deal with minor everyday illness and injuries, and are able to recognise when to seek assistance. Staff will also need to know how to access the trained first aiders.

The true case study outlined in Activity 5 Chapter 9, page 86, illustrates how easy it is for procedures to go wrong if they are unclear or unrehearsed. The learning points on page 87 may be helpful.

Fire procedures

Managers are often concerned that fire drill practice at lunchtime will be too disruptive. To overcome this problem you can set up a simulation at a different time of day.

Working with children who have special medical needs

This is discussed in Chapter 9, page 87, and in DfES 2005b.

Playground health and safety checklist

	Yes	No
Are LTSs offered health and safety training relevant to their role of supervising the playground?	☐	☐
Are children constructively occupied in the playground and are LTSs actively encouraged to supervise and interact with them?	☐	☐
Are there flat roofs or other dangerous structures which children climb on?	☐	☐
Are there hidden areas of the playground which are under-supervised?	☐	☐
Are regular risk assessments made of playground activities?	☐	☐
Are LTSs included in health and safety reviews and risk assessment of playground activities?	☐	☐
Are the playground rules outlining acceptable behaviour clear and on display?	☐	☐
Is there sufficient shade in the playground to protect children from the sun?	☐	☐
Are there adequate numbers of working water fountains?	☐	☐
Are the playground floor surfaces and equipment inspected on a regular basis?	☐	☐
Does the playground have insecure boundaries or public access? If so are there adequate measures in place to ensure staff and		

children's safety? □ □

Do members of staff park cars in the playground and if so is this managed adequately? □ □

Are parents/carers regularly reminded about the school's expectations concerning playground safety? □ □

Are children encouraged to understand the consequences of play behaviour and the nature of risk? □ □

Are all members of the school community including the children encouraged to share some responsibility for health and safety? □ □

Are there clear procedures for dealing with both minor and more serious accidents and emergencies in the playground? □ □

Supervising the school building during lunchtime checklist

Is behaviour in the dining room well managed? □ □

Are there clear dining room rules on display? □ □

Are children clear about the rules and routines for moving around the school and dining room at lunchtime? □ □

During wet play are there sufficient numbers of LTSs to supervise the classrooms and the dining room? □ □

Are risk assessments regularly made of wet play activities? □ □

Are classes ever left alone during wet play even for brief periods of time? □ □

Is wet play equipment checked on a regular basis? □ □

Are LTSs encouraged to plan and monitor wet play activities to minimise risk? □ □

Are children ever given permission to be inside the school building at lunchtime without the LTSs' knowledge? □ □

Are all lunchtime staff clear on fire procedures including how to evacuate the building and activate the fire alarm? □ □

Is the fire drill practised during lunchtime? □ □

Are there clear procedures for dealing with both minor and more serious accidents that occur in the school building during lunchtime? □ □

Chapter 10 Child protection

Support staff work closely with children and so may be in the front line in detecting child abuse. They will need to receive training and support to ensure that they are able to recognise and respond to concerns appropriately.

Chapter 10 discusses what constitutes abuse and who abuses children. It briefly outlines relevant child protection law and what is likely to happen when the social services department becomes involved. The chapter focuses in greater detail on how LTSs can recognise signs of abuse and how best they can respond to protect children. It also looks at their professional conduct and how to minimise the risk of false accusations.

Guidance for schools

Safeguarding Children in Education (DfES 2004) outlines the roles and responsibilities of the LEAs, the governing bodies and the head teacher. It also includes a useful summary of relevant guidance and legislation (see DfES 2004, Appendix 1, page 31–2).

Training for support staff

Government guidelines state that LEAs are expected to provide child protection induction training for all new staff who work with children. This can include written guidance. Schools are required to give all staff who work with children a written statement about the school's policy and procedures, and the name and contact details of the 'designated person'. Schools may also decide to offer LTSs school-based child protection training.

LTSs will need to know how to:

- Recognise the signs of child abuse (see page 92).
- Listen and respond to children's disclosures (see pages 94–6 and DfES 2004, annex B, page 25).
- Respond to concerns about a child's well-being as outlined by the school child protection policy (see page 95 and DfES 2004).
- Behave professionally at work to protect themselves from accusations of abuse (see Chapters 5 and 10, and DfES 2004).

Other issues to be clarified include:

Confidentiality of information

Information about children who have been abused will be shared on a 'need to know' basis. As discussed in previous chapters, LTSs often request enough information to help them to do their job properly (see Chapter 2 and Chapter 10, page 92). LTSs will also benefit from guidance on how to respond to parents/carers that approach them to discuss confidential issues.

The duty to refer

This has been discussed in detail in Chapter 10, page 91. School procedures for referral may need clarification as in some teams LTSs are expected to refer concerns of abuse to the senior LTS, whereas in others it may be the senior designated teacher. LTSs will need to be encouraged to report their concerns no matter how confused or uncertain they may feel.

Professional conduct and appropriate physical contact

See DfES 1998a. This legislation is likely to be amended, which may have considerable implications for practice in schools. Appropriate physical contact has also been discussed in Chapter 5, page 52 and in Chapter 10, page 96.

A child protection checklist

Are LTSs...	Yes	No
offered appropriate training by the school or the LEA to enable them to recognise and respond to concerns about child abuse?	☐	☐
familiar with the school child protection policy and how it relates to their work with children?	☐	☐
updated on any changes in child protection procedures?	☐	☐
given a written statement about the school's policy and procedures and the name and contact details of the designated person in school?	☐	☐
clear who to refer concerns to, and how to follow procedures for recording incidents?	☐	☐
encouraged to talk about issues with an appropriate person, when they are feeling uncertain or confused?	☐	☐
offered appropriate feedback about child abuse concerns they have reported?	☐	☐
encouraged to listen to children in a non-judgemental and sensitive way?	☐	☐
aware of ways to respond when talking to children about suspected abuse?	☐	☐
clear that they cannot promise children confidentiality?	☐	☐
offered guidance about confidentiality of information including how best to respond to parents/carers who may approach them?	☐	☐
given guidance and opportunities to discuss appropriate physical contact with pupils?	☐	☐
offered guidelines about professional conduct to minimise the risk of false accusations of abuse being made against them?	☐	☐

LTS training and career development

We are now in a climate of lifelong learning in which people are encouraged to return to study at any stage of their life to gain skills and confidence to progress.

Appraisal and professional development reviews

Your school may have gained Investors In People status, and so will be required to plan for the continuous professional development of all staff – not just teachers. Some schools have introduced systems whereby LTSs are offered reviews to help focus on their own needs and development. This may be a formal appraisal, or a less formal professional development discussion.

Career development

Many LTSs are happy with their role. Others may choose to consider a range of career development options including obtaining qualifications to become a teaching assistant, welfare officer, playworker or a qualified first aider. There may be a range of administrative responsibilities available too.

Training options

After many years of being given a low priority, training for support staff is now being developed. This is partly in response to the workforce agreement which aims to reduce teachers' workloads. Schools are now delegating some of the administrative tasks which were previously undertaken by teachers to support staff and LTSs – see Notes for managers, page 110.

In many areas schools are being funded by the government under the Employer Training Pilot to offer low-skilled employees basic qualifications. There are a growing number of options available which you may wish to discuss with your line manager or training mentor (if your school has one in post). Some of these options will be explored below, and a number of useful organisations have been listed at the end of this section.

Courses run by your local education authority

Attending courses outside your school can offer the opportunity to share ideas and good practice with others. Courses for support staff will vary depending on which area of the UK you work in. Find out how this training is advertised so that you can keep up to date.

College courses

There is a large range of relevant courses offered by local colleges. You can usually obtain their prospectuses from the local library, or by contacting them directly.

Basic maths, English and computer skills

If you wish to improve your basic maths, English or computing skills, many local colleges offer level 1 and level 2 courses in numeracy, literacy and information and computer technology (ICT). These may involve attending a number of sessions at a college where you can do trial tests, and gain individual and/or group support. If you have access to a computer you can do a lot of the work online. To find out more, phone your local college or visit the Move On website www.move-on.org.uk. This offers free skills checks, refresher courses and a list of local centres where you can register for courses. If there is a group of staff wanting to gain these qualifications your school may be willing to organise teaching sessions at your workplace.

Accredited qualifications for support staff

In September 2005 the Training and Development Agency for schools (TDA) took on the wider role of working with schools to help them develop and train their whole school workforce including support staff. If you have access to a computer, you can visit their website to find out more about what is available on www.tda.gov.uk.

You can obtain a full list of accredited qualifications for support staff from the TDA website. There are a number of relevant Vocational Qualifications (VQs), National Vocational Qualifications (NVQs) or Scottish Vocational Qualifications (SVQs), which involve demonstrating that you are achieving a particular level of competence in the work you are doing.

Since September 2004 an award for support work in schools has been piloted all over the country. This is a level 2 or 3 accredited qualification with a deliberately flexible structure to allow schools and candidates to select units to match their specific jobs. The sessions are usually school-based to help participants to feel more comfortable in their surroundings. Once you have achieved this qualification you may choose to build on your learning to gain the equivalent of a level 2 NVQ.

If you are also working as a teaching assistant you can undertake a range of awards including the level 2 or 3 NVQ for teaching assistants. You can also discuss the possibility of being put forward to undertake the training to achieve the higher level teaching assistant status – see web address below.

Other useful contacts

The HLTA award
For details visit www.hlta.gov.uk

Learndirect
Advice service for people over 20 who have fewer than five GCSEs or an NVQ level 2.
www.learndirect-advice.co.uk or telephone 0800 100 900 to speak to an advisor.

Move On
www.move-on.org.uk

Skills4Schools
www.skills4schools.org.uk
Telephone 0207 551 1154
This is an online resource to help school staff access learning opportunities at work.
It was set up in October 2005 to help staff take advantage of new career opportunities
created by the workforce agreement.

Training and Development Agency
www.tda.gov.uk
Telephone 0845 606 0323

References and bibliography

Berger, Nan (1990) *The School Meal Service from its Beginning to the Present Day.* Tavistock: Northcote House Educational Publishers.

Blatchford, Peter (1998) *Social Life in Schools: Pupils' Experience of Breaktimes and Recess from 7–16.* London: Routledge.

British Heart Foundation (2001) *Active Playgrounds: Guide for Primary Schools.* Loughborough: BHF Publications.

Burnham, Louise and Jones, Helen (2002) *The Teaching Assistant's Handbook.* Oxford: Heinemann.

Byl, John (2003) 101 Fun Warm-Up and Cool-Down Games. Human Kinetics website www.humankinetics.com

ChildLine (2004) Racism information sheet from the ChildLine website www.childline.org.uk/

Children and Young People's Unit (2001) *Learning to Listen: Core Principles for the Involvement of Children and Young People.* London: CYPU.

Thomas Coram Research Unit (2003) *Tackling Bullying – Listening to the Views of Children and Young People.* London: DfES.

Department of Health (2003) *What to Do If You're Worried a Child Is Being Abused (summary).* London: Department of Health.

DfES (1995) Circular 10/95. London: DfES.

DfES (1998a) Circular 10/98. London: DfES.

DfES (1998b) *Guidance on First Aid for Schools: A Good Practice Guide.* Teachernet website www.teachernet.gov.uk

DfES (2001) *Health and Safety Responsibilities and Powers.* London: DfES.

DfES (2003) *Introductory Training for Support Staff.* London: DfES.

DfES (2004) *Safeguarding Children in Education.* Teachernet website www.teachernet.gov.uk

DfES (2005a) *Playtimes and Lunchtimes Primary National Strategy Professional Development Pack.* London: DfES.

DfES (2005b) *Managing Medicine in Schools and Early Years Settings.* Teachernet website www.teachernet.gov.uk

Dreikurs, Rudolf, Grunwald, Bernice and Pepper, Floy (1998) *Maintaining Sanity in the Classroom: Classroom Management Techniques.* New York: Taylor and Francis.

Elliot, Michelle (1994) *Keeping Safe: A Practical Guide to Talking to Children.* London: Coronet Books.

Golding, Rob (2000) *Playground Games; More Playground Games*. Cambridge: Pearson Publishing Group.

Jackson, Mary (2004) Quoted in David Bocking article 'Time for play', *TES* 8 October 2004.

Kumar, Lalit (1991) *Teaching in England: Awareness of Different Cultural Traits*. Teachernet website www.teachernet.gov.uk

Lloyd, Richard and Ching, Charlene (2003) *School Security Concerns*. Teachernet website www.teachernet.gov.uk

National Centre for Playwork Education (2000) *Everyone Can Play: Inclusive Play Training Pack*. Gloucestershire: National Centre Playwork Education South West.

Northern, Stephanie (2004) 'School grounds', *TES* 16 January 2004.

Ormrod, J.E. (1999) *Human Learning*, 3rd edn. Upper Saddle River, NJ: Prentice Hall.

Rogers, Bill (2003) *Behaviour Management: A Whole School Approach*. London: Paul Chapman.

Smith, Peter (2000) *Bullying – Don't Suffer in Silence: An Anti Bullying Pack for Schools*. www.dfes.gov.uk\bullying

Tauber, Robert T. (1997) *Self-Fulfilling Prophecy: A Practical Guide to its Use in Education*. Portsmouth: Greenwood Publishing Group.

Theory into practice database http://tip.psychology.org/behaviourism B.F. Skinner.

Thomson, Sarah (2003) 'A well equipped hamster cage: the rationalisation of primary school playtime', *Education 3–13*, June 2003.

Thomson, Sarah (2005) 'Territorialising the primary school playground: deconstructing the geography of playtime', *Children's Geographies*, 3 (1), pp. 63–78, April 2005.

Titman, Wendy (1992) *Play, Playtimes and Playgrounds*. Crediton: Southgate Publishers.

White, Angela and Wilkinson, Jane (2000) *Playtimes and Playgrounds*. Bristol: Lucky Duck.

Youth Sport Trust (2004) *Primary Playground Development Pack*. Loughborough: Youth Sport Trust.

Websites and useful contacts

Anti-Bullying Alliance
www.nch.org/aba
0207 843 6000

Anti-Bullying Campaign
0207 378 1446

Association of Play Industries provide a full list
www.playindustries.org
0204 7641 4999

Bullying Online
www.bullying.co.uk

Children's Play Council – children's play information service and the council for disabled children
www.ncb.org.uk
0207 843 6000

Collins, Wendy (1998) *Active Playtimes*
www.southgatepublishers.co.uk

Department for Culture, Media and Sport, *Zoneparcs Funding*
www.culture.gov.uk

Directory for Social Change.
See Fundraising for Schools
www.dsc.org.uk

Games Kids Play
www.gameskidsplay.net

Growing Schools
www.teachernet.gov.uk

Kidscape
www.kidscape.org.uk
0207 730 3300

Learning Through Landscapes
www.ltl.org.uk

Lottery Fund
www.community-fund.org.uk

Playground Pals
www.pioneer.cwc.net/playgroundpals.htm

Playwork training qualifications
www.playwork.org.uk
0207 632 2000

Rose, Shirley
www.shirleyrose.co.uk
shirley@crorose.eclipse.co.uk

Sabin, Val (2004) *Positive Play: An Activities Manual and Guide for Positive Play at Breaktime*
www.valsabinpublications.com
01604 580947

Index